PAUL OWEN

THE JOY OF RUNNING

Summersdale Publishers Ltd
46 West Street
Chichester
West Sussex
PO19 1RP
UK

www.summersdale.com

Printed and bound by CPI Group (UK) Ltd, Croydon, CRO 4YY

ISBN: 978-1-84953-458-1

Substantial discounts on bulk quantities of Summersdale books are available to corporations, professional associations and other organisations. For details contact Nicky Douglas by telephone: +44 (0) 1243 756902, fax: +44 (0) 1243 786300 or email: nicky@summersdale.com.

To Fiona, Megan and James.
Thank you for explaining apostrophes. My head hurts.
I'm going for a run.

CONTENTS

INTRODUCTION

You never forget your first time do you? Mine was a hot, sweaty affair at the seaside which lasted just over four hours and fourteen minutes that left me dehydrated, exhausted and totally smitten.

Blackpool Marathon took place in the middle of a heatwave at the height of summer on 19 June 2005, and I spent six months training, thinking about and preparing for the race. I still recall the feelings I had at the time, of excitement, anticipation, self-doubt and ultimately relief once I reached the finish line... oh, and the soreness that meant I could hardly walk for days. As soon as I could, the desire to repeat my brief encounter started leading to regular trips to the postbox with race-entry forms. Despite many subsequent wonderful running experiences, Blackpool will always stay with me as the place that I lost my marathon virginity.

The act of running has played a pivotal role in the evolution of humanity since the birth of mankind. It has been important to many different civilisations throughout the ages for a wide variety of reasons. Early hunters relied on foot power to support their carnivorous diet; armies deployed long-distance runners to relay messages; the Ancient Olympics was initially a religious festival combining ceremony and athletic endeavour; promoters staged races and charged the public to watch, and running was central to the development of a wide variety of sports such as rugby and football.

Running races of one form or other have been popular for thousands of years, and to this day continue to attract both professional and amateur athletes the world over. The growth of participants in organised races continues to spiral upwards, with today's runner being able to choose from pure athletic races, obstacle-based events or those that involve another sport, such as triathlons. We have the luxury of being able to pick and choose what we enter, where we go and how we get there. The Internet and budget airlines have contributed to the rise in the number of 'running tourists', who think nothing of hopping on a flight to another country just to enter a race, before returning to work the next day with their colleagues none the wiser. Closer to home, the parkrun phenomena has brought fun, free and pressure-less access to 5 k events up and down Britain.

The benefits of being a runner are vast. Not only can it aid weight loss and depression, assist with sleeping problems and extend life expectancy, it can also help us to escape momentarily from the pressures of life. It can lead to friendship, love and an improved sex life. Far from causing problems such as 'runner's knee', it can actually help prevent injury as bone density increases even in older athletes. It can take you to places that you might never have gone, and to see things that you might never have seen.

For me, that has meant watching the sun rise and fall from the side of mountains, experiencing the beauty of a trail run in every weather condition, discovering the stillness and peace of running throughout the night and early morning, marvelling in the wonder of nature and all its glory and, perhaps most importantly, reawakening a level of enjoyment for the sport that had been locked away for too many years; an enjoyment that can be shared with anyone who laces up a pair of running shoes and simply runs, no matter the distance, speed or terrain. I hope I can share that enjoyment with you.

Paul Owen, 2013

CHAPTER 1

A BRIEF HISTORY OF RUNNING

Every morning in Africa a gazelle wakes up. It knows it must move faster than the lion or it will not survive. Every morning a lion wakes up and it knows it must move faster than the slowest gazelle or it will starve. It doesn't matter if you are the lion or the gazelle, when the sun comes up, you better be moving.

ANONYMOUS

Runners that time forgot

Whilst Palaeolithic cave paintings don't depict early *Homo erectus* wearing the now-famous striped footwear of Mr Adi Dassler or the 'swoosh' design of a certain American  sports brand, science can tell that humans developed the ability to run primarily to survive. Before the invention of 24-hour convenience stores, foot power was the main way to catch prey or scavenge carcasses before other predators arrived on the scene. Science can't say for certain why pre-humans became bipedal and if the ability to run was a by-product of being able to walk upright on two limbs, or the central factor in the evolution of the human body as it is now. Nevertheless, once upright, *Homo erectus*, *neanderthalensis* and subsequently *sapiens* all used one of their greatest strengths to maintain a carnivorous protein-rich diet. Whilst never the fastest movers, they were capable in terms of endurance of eventually outrunning any animal on earth over a long distance, which remains the case to this day.

Depending upon which evolutionary camp your modern, well-cushioned foot is in, arguably humans' ability to run has led to every single advance and development in history. Running has been central to each civilisation that has ever existed, for a wide variety of survival, social and economic reasons. Artefacts from antiquity often depict humans running – for example, kylixes (slightly edgy wine-drinking cups), popular during the Mycenaean era in ancient Greece, had designs including naked warriors running into battle, which the drinker would not see until the content had been consumed.

One of the greatest battles in history took place at Marathon in 490 BC when the Persian King Darius I's army landed seeking to conquer Greece, coming toe to toe with the Athenians as they did so. During this period, *Hemerodromes* (day runners) were used widely to courier messages very long distances. Before the battle, a professional Greek messenger by the name Pheidippides is said to have run over 150 miles in 48 hours to seek help from Sparta for the Athenians, a feat which would go on to inspire the Spartathlon Ultra Race.

After the battle, he supposedly ran a further 26 miles to carry news of the victory to Athens, uttering on arrival, 'Joy to you, we've won', before promptly keeling over and dying from exhaustion. His exploits and death were recorded and passed down through the ages in various literary forms including a poem by Robert Browning which is believed to be the inspiration for Baron Pierre de Coubertin and fellow founders of the modern Olympic Games, to invent a race celebrating the achievements of the 40-year-old messenger, which they called the Marathon. By choosing that distance, the Baron and his chums also inadvertently and simultaneously created 'the wall' which, every marathoner will know, can happen around the 18 to 20-mile point as the body's energy sources start to run out of fuel. 'Why couldn't Pheidippides have died here?' an athlete named Frank Shorter is attributed to have said to a fellow runner Kenny Moore at the 16-mile point of one of his earliest marathons.

It's a question of sport

There is little historical evidence identifying when running for sport purposes first occurred. Races certainly took place in ancient Egypt even before the great pyramids were built and monuments to the pharaohs circa 2000 BC show various sports were up and running, including athletics. Pottery from ancient Greece also shows that running was used for both political and social reasons, depicting warriors sprinting into battle or shieldless men running for pleasure.

Certainly by the time of the birth of the Ancient Olympic Games in Olympia in 776 BC, the use of running as a spectacle had been established. The first Olympics was linked to religious festivals in honour of Zeus, King of the Gods, although races were not part of a particular ceremony. Initially there was one short sprint race of unclear length, with a second longer event introduced in 724 BC. Four race distances were eventually added to the schedule. The final one, called a *Hoplitodromos*, required competitors to carry a shield and armour.

King Tahaka instituted a 100 k race for his Egyptian soldiers between 690 and 665 BC, which has been recreated in the 100 k Pharaonic Race. Hieroglyphics from the time suggest the king himself took part.

As race clocks and timing systems hadn't been invented, the precise times of the first Olympians are not known, although the results are. Léonidas of Rhodes was the Usain Bolt of his day, winning three races in the 164 BC games and repeating the feat in the three games that followed. Both Léonidas and Bolt have been declared the greatest sprinters of all time and reaped the rewards. Léonidas picked up an olive branch and the adulation of the country. Bolt picked up £13 million in 2012, made 63rd place on Forbes' The World's Highest-Paid Athletes list and has the adulation of pretty much every athletics fan on the planet.

In Britain, a hill race took place in Braemar, Scotland, circa 1040 and similar events appear sporadically in the years that followed. In Italy, the Palio del Drappo Verde foot race, of approximately 10 km in length, reportedly dates back to 1208 and continues to this day. The Red Hose Run 3 k was first held in Carnwath, Scotland, in 1509 under a royal charter from King James IV. The race has been run 491 times since and is still going strong.

I'll have a guinea on my man

By the sixteenth century, cross-country running was a part of English public school life, with its emphasis on outdoor activity being good for the mind and the body. Events such as Paper Chase (or Hare and Hounds) involved a lead runner known as the 'hare' laying a trail of paper for the 'hounds' to follow and would eventually lead to the formation of gentlemen's running clubs incorporating 'hare and hounds', or 'harriers', in their names. These schools could only be accessed by the wealthy, and the instilling of athletics into impressionable young minds partly explains the popularity of the rich placing large wagers on their man servants in specifically designed events of huge distances. Excessive gambling occurred in a wide variety of sports and athletics did not go untouched, despite the attempts of the authorities through laws such as the Gaming Act 1664. Over the course of the next few centuries, professional runners would become commonplace.

Professional runners

John Bryant in *The London Marathon* recounts the case of Captain Robert Barclay Allardice who, for a 1,000-guinea wager in 1809, covered 1,000 miles in 1,000 consequetive hours at no more than one mile per hour. A runner named Moorex 'the Italian giant', repeated the feat in1862 from Warren House, Lindley Moor in West Yorkshire. Bryant and London Marathon director Dave

Bedford thought it would be fun to recreate the attempt over seven weeks before the 2002 race. Five of the six starters finished, with the winner netting a hefty cheque.

By the 1870s, six-day races on indoor tracks with substantial prize money on offer were quite commonplace. In 1878, a series of five international six-day events was created. In 1882 in Madison Square Garden, George Hazael became the first man to run 600 miles in six days.

Amateur Athletic Association (AAA)

In response to the growing number of professional races, the AAA was inaugurated in the Randolph Hotel, Oxford, in 1880 to protect the amateur principles of clubs including the university's athletic club, Thames Hare & Hounds (formed in 1868) and clubs that followed such as Ranelagh Harriers (formed in 1881). The AAA promoted the purity of running for the act itself rather than for any form of financial gain. This ethos brought it into direct opposition with promoters who created large-scale events with prize money, aimed at the public's desire for a flutter. The conflict between professional runners and their gentleman counterparts remained well after the formation of the AAA.

The wealthier amateurs may not have needed the prize money to buy the Xbox equivalent of the day, but runners such as builder Len Hurst did. He won the first professionally staged 40 k marathon in 1896 between Paris and Conflans in 2:31:30. Just two months after the first time the race had been run in the modern Olympics, Len beat Spyridon Louis' record of 2:58:50. It's not known if his speed was developed as a result of a long history of escaping disgruntled clients.

The professionals ran for prize money and tended to train harder than amateurs, for whom it was important to be seen to be winning without trying. This attitude is perfectly captured in the fact-based film, *Chariots of Fire*. Harold Abrahams was an amateur who tried to break the mould. He used a professional coach, Sam Mussabini, to help him win the 1924 Olympic 100 m – a tactic that for amateurs was years ahead of its time. It is now standard amongst professional athletes on all continents and yet, back then, it flew in the face of the amateur ethos, which arguably held the sport back for much of the first half of the twentieth century. Fortunately, for modern runners, Abrahams' views prevailed and through lifelong commitment to the sport, he changed the face of British athletics and its laws forever, eventually ascending to the giddy heights of chair of the AAA.

Play not only keeps us young but also maintains our perspective about the relative seriousness of things. Running is play, for even if we try hard to do well at it, it is a relief from everyday cares.

JIM FIXX, *THE COMPLETE BOOK OF RUNNING*

Across the pond, the first Trans-American Footrace started on the 4 March 1928, with 199 people trying to run 3,422 miles between the Ascot Speedway, Los Angeles, and Madison Square Garden, New York, for a prize of $25,000 – more than 16 times the average income at the time. Fifty-five would finish, with the winner Andy Payne crossing the line after 573 hours, 4 minutes and 34 seconds. Phew.

In 1970, the Big Apple staged its first marathon with 127 runners paying a $1 entry fee. Fifty-five of the intrepid gathering finished, spearheading a people's running revolution, which spread to almost every corner of the globe. When Fred Lebow organised that first race, it's doubtful he would have foreseen the millions worldwide who would subsequently take up the call to legs with such gusto.

The boom led to exercise disciples such as Jim Fixx. His book, *The Complete Book of Running*, was published in 1977, stayed at the top of the bestsellers list for two years and sold over a million copies, making him the go-to running guru of the decade. His status was cemented with *Jim Fixx's Second Book of Running*. Unfortunately for Jim, he died of a heart attack aged just 52 whilst out running. The anti-running crowd had a field day at the irony of his death, through what was actually a degenerative heart condition that could just have easily hit on a Saturday night in front of *Kojak*. His books are still on sale to this day – a popular tool amongst runners the world over – answering the detective's infamous line, 'Who loves ya, baby?'

The current state of affairs

By the time of Fixx's premature passing, running as a recreational pastime was firmly established. Throughout the 1980s, many half and full marathons were created all over the world. It became de rigueur for any big city of note to have a major road race, dipping into the seemingly bottomless pockets of the new wave of runners in search of adventure and travel.

In 1986, the Bay to Breakers 12.01 k/7.46-mile race was accredited by the Guinness World Records as the largest foot race ever, with over 110,000 starters, until it was surpassed by the 10.10.10 Run for the Pasig River in the

Philippines with 116,086 finishers. The former remains the site for the World Centipede Running Championships. The New York City Marathon had 47,340 finishers in 2011, also a world record, and both records are likely to be extended in years to come. Whilst average race times are down on those of the flared-trousers era, participation in races is significantly higher with many races sold out within hours of their opening.

The spread of the non-professional running phenomena shows no signs of abating. A cursory glance at *Runner's World* reveals some form of race every single weekend in the UK and these continue to evolve to meet the differing needs of the thousands of runners who take part in them. Whatever form of running experience you are looking for, it is out there – along with some you probably wouldn't even have thought about. There has never been a more exciting time for non-professional runners than right now.

> *On 28 April 2013, around 5,000 runners entered the Marathon of the North, which combined half and full-marathon distances. Only one runner finished either race. The second and third-placed runners lost sight of the leader Mark Hood, went the wrong way and took the entire field of runners with them, who were all subsequently disqualified.*

CHAPTER 2

WHY DO WE RUN?

Running, one might say, is basically an absurd pastime upon which to be exhausting ourselves. But if you can find meaning in the type of running you need to do ... chances are you'll be able to find meaning in that other absurd pastime – life.

Bill Bowerman, coach

Is there one reason?

Running means freedom, pure and simple. The 24/7 demands of modern society, emails, smartphones and social media, mean for many there is little escape from work, financial worries or advertisers preaching a message that life is just not good enough without the latest must-have gadget. And that's why, in our consumer-driven society, running has never been more popular – or more important. Running is a positive way of releasing pent-up emotions. It is cheap, accessible and, apart from basic running gear, only needs terra firma on which to run, anywhere in the world at any time. Running is pure escapism and can become addictive – if you are lucky.

The healthy option

For many the number one reason to first pull on the Lycra is health. Countless studies around the world have proven how beneficial running is in reducing blood pressure, bad cholesterol, improving heart strength and facilitating weight loss. It is one of the quickest ways to improve levels of cardiovascular fitness, especially in those runners just starting out. The fitter they become, the further and quicker they go. Those trails close to home never before ventured along will become playgrounds. Car journeys will involve new trail-spotting opportunities and noting of cemeteries with flowers – the churches tend to have outside taps, essential on a hot summer run. 'Running is my church', said the actress Joan Van Ark, although she didn't mention plumbing.

Running improves self-esteem through weight loss, goal setting and a sense of achievement. It can help concentration, beat insomnia and even improve eyesight. It can bring new friends, adventure and travel. Ordinary Joes can dream of emulating the feats of athletic superstars like Scott Jurek and Michael Johnson, or singer David Lee Roth of Van Halen fame who ran the New York City Marathon in a little over six hours. Ordinary Josephine's can follow in the same footsteps as Helene Diamantides, Liz Yelling or Sally Gunnell.

Sports such as bodybuilding might create a Charles Atlas physique, but don't go after visceral fat coating rather important organs. Even the dark art of cycling involves sitting down for, well, all of the time. Running combines the use of large muscle groups and the need to support body weight, which helps to burn fat for up to 14 hours after an average 45-minute run because of the boost it gives to the body's metabolic rate. Combine running with friends, a trip to the seaside for a 10 k run and an extra-large Mr Whippy – once the weight is off – and life can hardly get better. For the more adventurous, follow coach Bart Yasso's example (the inventor of the Yasso 800s training technique) and race on all seven continents, or Ron Hill's and compete in races in 100 countries around the world. But then Great Yarmouth is likely to be a tad cheaper.

Death and runner's knee

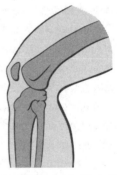

The certainties of the runner's life and reasons not to run, right? Far from it. There are high-profile cases where death and running have tragically collided, as we've seen with Fixx and Pheidippides. At the 1912 Olympic marathon in Stockholm, Francisco Lázaro collapsed in the race and died the next day from heatstroke. Deaths have also occurred during amateur races and, in most cases, the act of running hasn't caused the death. Clinical studies have shown that deaths in under-35s are more likely to be due to congenital heart defects and over that age to heart degeneration, such as in the case of Fixx, whose pre-running obesity and heavy smoking caught up with him.

A study over 15 years by the University of South Carolina reported a 19 per cent lower risk of death in runners compared with non-runners. For the majority, the simple act of running can extend their mobility over sedentary people by up to 16 years, increase life spans by a whopping 6.2 years for men and 5.6 years for women, and cut the risk of chronic diseases such as Alzheimer's by up to 20 per cent. While running doesn't prevent the inevitable, it can for many help to push it back for many years. No argument really.

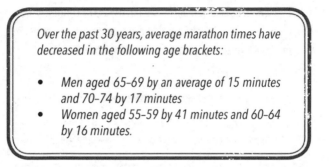

Over the past 30 years, average marathon times have decreased in the following age brackets:

- *Men aged 65–69 by an average of 15 minutes and 70–74 by 17 minutes*
- *Women aged 55–59 by 41 minutes and 60–64 by 16 minutes.*

Non-runners invariably point to the joints of their active friends as an excuse not to take up the hobby. Injuries occur and runner's knee – or patellofemoral pain syndrome – is an occupational hazard, as are other overuse-related problems (such as the dreaded plantar fasciitis, which causes pain in the heel or bottom of the foot). In an active sport, these are to be expected, but in the longer term, runners' bone density can increase, lowering the risk of fractures. One study by the University of Missouri compared the skeletal density of runners and cyclists. It found that 63 per cent of cyclists had low mineral density in their hips and spines, compared with 19 per cent of runners. Running can help slow the speed at which muscle mass is lost by the body in the ageing process, even in those taking up the sport well into their 70s and 80s.

Participation in running events is on the increase among older runners whose knees seem equal to the task. Take Dave Sedgley of Ampthill and Flitwick Flyers, a septuagenarian who has run over a hundred marathons and continues to enter 100-mile challenge events. Alternatively, Iva Barr of Bedford Harriers, an octogenarian who first entered the London Marathon in 1982, carried the Olympic torch in 2012 and was the oldest female finisher in the 2013 London Marathon with a time of 6:37:57. Even Arnold Schwarzenegger has swapped at least one bench-pressing session for a bit of roadwork of late.

> On 21 April 2013, 88-year-old Paul Freedman finished the London Marathon in a time of 7:41:33.

Weighty issues

Born-again runners Neale and Emma Else previously weighed a combined 44 st 6 lbs. An ordinary couple from suburbia, Neale tipped the scales at 20 st 8 lbs and was heading for an early meeting with his maker – but Emma was in the lead in that race,  coming in at 23 st 12 lbs. The running bug took a while to grow, as they struggled with gym equipment behind closed doors to lose enough weight before pounding the pavements. Neale began running at night when he thought no one was around. At that stage, it was just a means to an end and not the all-encompassing lifestyle that either of them could have contemplated would happen. As Neale says, 'I used to watch the London Marathon with envy and think that I could never run for so long. How wrong was I? I run to train and I run for fun and I run to enjoy a beer and a curry without feeling guilty.' In less than two years, Emma dropped to 9 st 12 lbs and Neale to 13 st 7 lbs. Both are now accomplished runners and have completed various race distances including, in Neale's case, the Milton Keynes Marathon on two occasions.

> *A commonly held runner's view is that for every pound of weight lost, 2 seconds per mile are saved in a marathon; 10 lbs lost can mean more than a minute quicker in a 5 k run and more than nine minutes in a marathon. The theory works for many.*

Wil Graham, a contestant on the reality show *The Biggest Loser*, lost 8 st 7 lbs to win the show, eventually going from 29 st 6 lbs to under 15 st. Along the way, he discovered a love of running and bagged a half-marathon time of 2:20 at Reading in 2011. He needed to lose weight before he could run, but having done so he has used the sport to stop the pounds from piling back on. Graham discovered that running isn't a chore, to be undertaken for a specific goal and then forgotten. For these people and many more like them, running has changed their lives, provided new challenges and delayed them reaching the ultimate finishing line. That's one timing mat they are happy not to cross.

More sex, please, we're British

'Running is my lover.'
TOSHIHIKO SEKO, ATHLETE

To London Marathon winners running might be their lover, but to other people running can improve their sexual health: for men, it's great for vascular health, impotence and erectile dysfunction, particularly in the over-50 age bracket, according to one Harvard study. For women, it's even better news. Israeli physician Alexander Olshanietzky said before the 1996 Olympics, 'Women get better results in sports competition after orgasm... the more orgasms, the more chances of winning a medal.' Boxer Rocky Balboa's coach might have told the champ, 'Women weaken the legs', but it's debatable how many athletes follow that advice the night before a big race. Who's right? No idea, but it's fun trying to find out.

CHAPTER 3

TRAINING

*Now, here, you see, it takes all the running you can do to
keep in the same place. If you want to get somewhere
else, you must run at least as twice as fast as that!*

LEWIS CARROLL, *THROUGH THE LOOKING-GLASS*

To plan or not to plan?

Herb Elliott had the guidance of Percy Cerutty, Mo Farah has Alberto
Salazar and Paula Radcliffe has Gary Lough. Recreational runners
don't have the luxury of one-to-one mentors. Nevertheless, copying
the training plans of the pros could reap rewards for any runner. The
pros gradually increase their training over a year with a period of base
strengthening work, picking times to peak, following basic training
methods and building in recovery periods.

Unless you are on a daily running streak that began on 20
December 1964 like Ron Hill, rest is as crucial to progression as the
training techniques below. Training plans can be downloaded from
the Internet and adapted to ordinary runner's lives, who may have
to fit in long training runs in the dark before a day's work. No matter
if it's a 5 k race, marathon or simply running to get fitter, following a
structured training regime could reap rewards.

Training should be varied, involving different types of sessions and running speeds. Athletes aim for only two or three hard sessions each week, mixing in between slower-paced recovery runs.

Basic training sessions

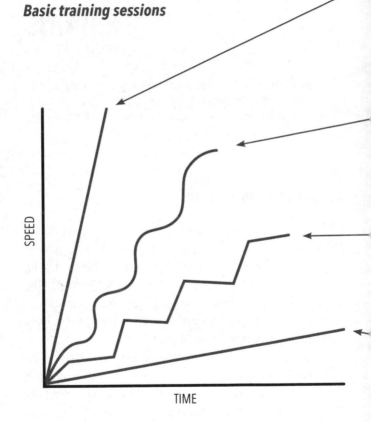

SPEED

TIME

Tempos (aka lactate threshold or threshold runs) – runs of 2 miles (3.2 km) or more at a pace where conversation is only just manageable. This develops an overall faster base pace as metabolic fitness is improved and the body adapts to using oxygen more efficiently. Everyone from a parkrunner to an ultrateer will benefit from a true tempo session. The session was popularised by coach Jack Daniels and, given he has a PhD in exercise physiology, I'd say he's worth listening to.

Fartleks – rather than being a reference to Nordic flatulence, the Swedish word meaning 'speed play' is a non-rigid training device created by coach Gösta Holmér for world-class runners like Gunder Hägg and Arne Andersson. Running speed is altered over varying distances, the objective being to run faster in short repeated bursts. The fitter the athlete, the more repetitions they will undertake.

Repetitions with intervals – another form of speed training in which intensity is near to maximum over shorter periods of ideally three to five minutes. A typical session involves three minutes of hard running, with a recovery of half the effort, repeated perhaps six to eight times. These will raise a runner's lactic threshold.

LSD – not an illicit hallucinogenic substance, the initials stand for 'long slow distance'. A foundation stone for runners of any distance, although the number-one training tool for long-distance bods. Praised as the best running coach of all time by *Runner's World*, New Zealander Arthur Lydiard believed in base-building endurance through repeated LSD runs. He would insist that his athletes covered at least 100 miles (161 km) a week in training, even 800 m runners such as Peter Snell who won gold at the 1960 Rome and 1964 Tokyo Olympics.

Which twitcher are you?

Everyone's a twitcher. Long-distance runners need slow-twitch muscle fibres; sprinters need fast-twitch fibres designed for explosive, rapid action, which tire quickly. By the end of a 100 m race, even Bolt is slowing down. He just slows down a little less quickly than the others around him. Whilst scientists believe a small percentage of the body's fibres can be trained, an athlete's muscle fibre is mainly genetically inherited through their ancestors. This is one of the factors that might help explain why peoples such as the Tarahumara or athletes in East Africa do well at distance running, while many sprinters can trace their lineage to West Africa whose people were spread across the globe by the slave trade.

The heart of the matter

When running, the heart increases the number of beats over its resting rate as the body absorbs oxygen into the blood. Runners benefit from increased cardiac output, which is the amount of oxygen-rich blood that travels from the heart, through tiny capillaries to the muscles. The more the heart is able to pump, the less it is strained.

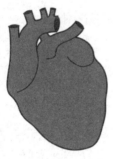

Regular, consistent training can help develop a stronger heart when combined with changes in lifestyle, such as giving up a pre-existing nicotine habit or changing a diet rich in high saturated fatty foods. Trained athletes usually have significantly lower resting heart rates than the wider population. While that isn't a guarantee against heart problems, it puts a runner on the right side of the risk divide. In the 1980 Moscow Olympics, runner Sebastian Coe was rumoured to have a resting heart beat of 28 bpm and a sustained heart rate of 250 bpm when running. Compare that with a healthy adult whose bpm is in the 60-80 range and it's no wonder he won gold.

Sleep

Tired people can crave chocolate. Less than six hours sleep per night means that the body is likely to produce increased levels of the hunger hormone ghrelin. Ideally runners  should aim to clock eight to ten hours' shut-eye in order to maintain a good metabolic rate, allow muscles to repair, and still have time to dream of standing on the winners' podium, flag raised and national anthem being sung.

Fringe benefits

Professional athletes like Kílian Jornet Burgada can eat whatever and whenever they want. If you are running 140 miles (225 km) a week and entering ultras all over the world it's not a problem. For the weekend athlete, however, it is. Running  isn't a passport to weight loss and deep-fried Mars Bars (they do exist and taste lovely). If the aim is to shed a few pounds, a runner should avoid too many high-calorie sports drinks or fatty foods. Fish and chips might have worked for comic book running legend Alf Tupper and his Greystone Harriers pals, but it's unlikely to work for other aspiring 'toughs of the track' if every run is rewarded with a high-calorie treat.

When body mass is reduced, VO_2 max is increased. This is the amount of oxygen consumed per kilogram of body weight. The lighter the runner, the further and faster they are likely to go. So, the bad news is, to get speedy, the fry-ups have to be shelved. The good news is that another study found a 45-minute workout could boost metabolic rate for up to 14 hours. That's not to say a blowout shouldn't happen. On the contrary – life is for living and when a particular race has been run, or a milestone reached, being able to tuck into a guilt-free slice of something naughty is nigh on mandatory.

Thomas Hicks won the 1904 St Louis Olympic marathon, during which he consumed doses of strychnine sulphate (common rat poison at the time) mixed with brandy; due to the choice of race hydration his trainers had to help him across the line, although he was not disqualified as Dorando Pietri was four years later.

In vino veritas

Excessive alcohol use and mile munching don't easily mix. Alcohol is a diuretic and causes dehydration with resulting pit stops during races. The heart has to work harder to supply blood to the muscles, causing fatigue, and the body's heat regulator – sweating – will be affected. So, does a life of teetotalism beckon the runner? Well, no. In moderation, red wine might help the production of a healthy heart chemical called resveratrol, which inhibits the development of fat cells around the waist and aids respiration. António Pinto, the Portuguese three-time winner of the London Marathon, advocated drinking red wine and even bought a vineyard.

The organisers of the Berlin Marathon give runners a glass of *alkoholfrei* beer at the finish, which doesn't taste nearly as nice as the real thing likely to be consumed with a bratwurst not long after. The Médoc Marathon in France provides runners and boozers with the opportunity to combine both cultures. Limited to 8,500 entrants, 90 per cent of whom will be in fancy dress, the race began in 1984 and should be on every runner's to-do list. It has 52 entertainment events along the route and 22 refreshment stops serving wine, oysters, ham, cheese and ice cream. Finishers receive a bottle of vino in the bulging goody bag. Personal-best hunters are discouraged, serious athletes frowned upon and personal-worst times are the norm. With all that food and wine, the challenge is to finish, let alone worry about time, which chances are will be forgotten the next day anyway. Adding the odd alcholic beverage to a training plan in moderation is fine, albeit abstinence in the week before a race is recommended even for those attempting the Médoc.

CHAPTER 4

GEAR AND GADGETS

*A Dandy is a clothes-wearing Man, a Man whose trade,
office and existence consists in the wearing of clothes.*

THOMAS CARLYLE, *SARTOR RESARTUS*

Gear and gadgets are essential, right?

Flying legal eagle Adam Campbell gained a Guinness World Record
for running the fastest marathon in a suit in a time of 2:35:51 at
Canada's Victoria Marathon in 2012, eclipsing the record formerly
held by Brit Paul Buchanan of 3:24:46, set in Dublin in 2009. Not
known for their wicking propensities, a three piece is not the athletic
clothing of choice for most. Modern sports technology has led to
major advances in the type of clothing and running-related gadgets
that are available to recreational and professional athletes alike.
Absorbent materials like cotton, which becomes heavy, wet and clingy
with perspiration, have been replaced with synthetic materials that
help moisture evaporate quicker, although can still lead to runner's
nipple without a liberal coating of Vaseline.

A well-known photograph of Dorando Pietri being helped across the finishing line of the 1908 Olympic marathon shows him wearing baggy clothing. Compression clothing for almost every part of the body has been developed since. Satellite navigation watches, nutrition bars, gels, miniature personal music devices, smartphones with downloadable applications and all manner of paraphernalia including bumbags, hydration rucksacks, Anti Monkey Butt Powder to avoid chafing and Shewees are now in many sports bags. It's a wonder how Pietri ever made it across the finish line. (Oh, that's right, he was helped and disqualified.)

> *Keith Levasseur ran Baltimore Marathon in 2012 in a time of 2:46:58 wearing flip-flops, earning himself a Guinness World Record. Other world records include Naomi Garrick who ran the London Marathon in 2012 wearing a wedding dress in 3:41:40; Andy McMahon in 3:28:38 in a gas mask; and Sasha Kenney in 5:05:57 running with a hula hoop.*

To shoe or not to shoe – bless you

Homo erectus was the pioneer of the barefoot running craze long before Abebe Bikila won the Rome Olympic marathon shoeless in 1960. His world record time of 2:15:16 stood as a barefoot record until 1978 when it was beaten by

India's Shivnath Singh, in Jalandhar, in a time of 2:12:00. Other shoeless devotees are athletes Bruce Tulloh, Zola Budd and the Tarahumara tribe in Mexico highlighted by Christopher McDougall in *Born to Run*. Early runners were saved a few shillings, but over the past few thousand millennia the training shoe industry has grown to an estimated £3.2 billion. The now-omnipresent global sports goods titans have shoes designed to meet the complex needs of the 33 joints, 26 bones and more than 100 ligaments, muscles and tendons which make up the foot.

I prefer running without shoes. My toes didn't get cold. Besides, if I'm in front from the start, no one can step on them.

MICHELLE DEKKERS, CROSS-COUNTRY RUNNER

The runner is faced with a dazzling and confusing array of training shoes to meet intricate and different needs. Pronation, overpronation and supination running styles are catered for in minimalist, neutral, motion control, cushioned, barefoot or performance shoes for trail, track, road and every surface save the moon, although that is just a matter of time. Most manufacturers change their shoes with each new athletic season, often with little obvious change to even the most committed fan other than cosmetic. The super powers know that once within their fold, repeat business (as shoes are worn out and replaced) is as certain as death and taxes. Once the right pair of shoes is found, it takes an event of seismic proportions to persuade a runner to move away from them.

New runners should have their running gait expertly assessed and avoid buying shoes that look the best in the shop. That doesn't mean spending a fortune, but rather finding the right fit for their specific foot. A study at the University of Bern in Switzerland, published recently in *Medicine & Science in Sports & Exercise*, assessed 4,358 runners. It concluded that athletes with shoes costing more than $95, with features such as extra cushioning, were twice as likely to be injured at some point than those with shoes costing less than half. One size does not fit all.

Satellite-navigation devices

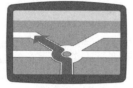

One of the most important advances for runners in the past 20 years has been the availability to the mass market of good quality, portable, accurate satellite-navigation watches incorporating all manner of data. They record the distance run, cycled or swum, time, average speed, route, calories burnt and heart rate, and even provide virtual running partners to race or train with. Runs can be uploaded and shared instantly via the Internet. Garmin was one of the first companies to grab a wristhold in the watch market in 1990 and has since produced market-leading devices. The name of the company is now as synonymous with speed and distance monitors as Kleenex is with tissues. By 2010, Garmin's early highly functional watches, which resembled small bricks, had been replaced by models such as the 110, which looks like, well, a normal watch.

> *Make running a habit. Set aside a time solely for running.*
> *Running is more fun if you don't have to rush through it.*
> JIM FIXX

Like the march of the penguins, runners can become focused on destinations and goals; they love numbers. Time, distance run, speed, elevation and descent are eagerly dissected and analysed. The target of a new personal best or finishing position in a race can detract from the joy of the journey. It's unlikely penguins on their treks will pull up and check out the views, but runners should. The use of GPS watches and the focus on the data they create can detract from the very thing an athlete enjoys in the first place, which is the simple act of pulling on their gear and heading out of the door for a run.

Watches and measurement devices play an important role in keeping the athlete honest in their ability. They should not, however, be allowed to detract from the beauty of an early-morning cross-country run when most people are just waking up, or cause an athlete to become too fixated on the numbers to the detriment of the reasons that brought them to the sport in the first place.

An advocate of running without devices was the late ultra runner Micah True, or Caballo Blanco as he became known to the native Tarahumara tribe in Mexico, who became famous through *Born to Run*. Born Michael Randall Hickman in Oakland, California, in 1953, True championed the enjoyment and the act itself of running over time and speed.

A healthy balance between the use of all the top-of-the-range gadgets and running without any could lead to longer-term running careers for non-professional athletes. There will inevitably be periods when motivation drops. A blast of The Rolling Stones, as favoured by Phil Hewitt in *Keep on Running*, might make the difference between a six miler and another slice of pizza. Better still, put the miles in and have a guilt-free slice after the run. Another option is to run and eat pizza at the same time, as ultra running legend Dean Karnazes did at midnight on Highway 116 in Napa Valley, California, in the middle of a 150-mile-plus training run. He opted for a large with all the trimmings.

Music on the run

Rhodesian-based English runner Arthur Newton won the Comrades Marathon in Durban, South Africa, five times and set a host of records in races, including the 100-mile London to Bath race and other 24-hour events in the 1930s. His racing plans included the use of a large gramophone. Whereas a spot of swing from Satchmo  might have helped Newton, for the next 40 years he would be in a minority of runners who could use music to their advantage. The Sony Walkman was the first portable personal music device to hit the masses and it transformed the way people trained. A bulky boxed cassette player strapped to the waist, it allowed a small number of songs to be listened to while running, allowing the user into imagine they were running up the steps of the Philadelphia Museum of Art like boxer Rocky Balboa, whilst pumping out 'Eye of the Tiger' for the fourth time. The development of the iPod and other small devices now allows a thousand songs to be taken on a run.

Studies have shown that upbeat music may help a runner clock faster times as they train to the beat, block out negative thoughts and experience increased blood flow, which helps to disperse lactic acid build up. On the flipside, another study conducted over a period of six years reported a 300 per cent increase in serious injuries to pedestrians wearing headphones. In 2007, the New York City Marathon banned the use of headphones through fear of injuries and most major races are now following suit.

776 BC	Competitors in the ancient games run barefoot
c.534 BC	An Etruscan attaches lower and upper parts of a sandal with metal tacks
490 BC	Pheidippides runs an ultra, picking up a few blisters
341 BC	Etruscan invention takes off
1830	An athletic shoe made from canvas and rubber is invented
1832	Wait Webster patents a design attaching rubber to shoes and boots (and creates the 'sneek thief', as the shoes were so quiet)
1854	Boots and shoes with spikes are developed
1870	John Boyd Dunlop invents plimsolls, later called Green Flash
1890s	Spiked running shoes sold by J.W. Foster & Sons (which later becomes Reebok)
1916	Keds trainer called Champion created with rubber sole
1924	Foster's supplies the shoes for the British Olympic team
1936	Adi Dassler supplies shoes to Jesse Owens
1948	Adidas formed by Adi Dassler and Puma by Rudolf Dassler

1952	Josy Barthel wears Puma shoes to win gold in the 1,500 m at Helsinki Olympics
1960	New Balance create a shoe with a wedged heel
1968	Tommie Smith wears Puma Suedes in 200 m at Mexico Olympics
1968	Smith and John Carlos remove their shoes for the medal ceremony
1971	Nike pays Carolyn Davidson $35 for her 'swoosh' design
1973	Steve Prefontaine endorses Nike and wears the company's shoes
1974	Nike launches its 'Waffle' shoe design
1975	Brooks uses EVA foam to lighten its shoes
1985	Asics introduces a gel cushioning system
2005	Vibram introduces FiveFingers shoes – mimicking barefoot running – and the rest try to catch up
2008	Haile Gebrselassie runs a new world record of 2:03:59 at the Berlin Marathon, wearing Adidas Daybreaks
2012	Usain Bolt runs into the history books at the London Olympics wearing Puma spikes
2017	Barefoot running takes over and the circle of life starts again

Rocking runners

- *Sean Combs (aka Puff Daddy, Diddy, P. Diddy), 2003 New York City Marathon (4:14:54)*
- *Flea (Red Hot Chili Peppers), 2011 Los Angeles Marathon (3:53:00)*
- *Nick Hexum (311), 2006 Los Angeles Marathon (5:29:44)*
- *Björn Ulvaeus (ABBA), 1980 Stockholm Marathon (3:23:54)*
- *Ronan Keating (Boyzone), 2008 London Marathon (3:59:44)*
- *Mike Malinin (Goo Goo Dolls), 2000 San Francisco Marathon (3:23:56)*
- *Alanis Morissette, 2009 Bizz Johnson Trail Marathon (4:17:03)*
- *David Lee Roth (Van Halen), 2010 New York City Marathon (6:04:43)*
- *Joe Strummer (The Clash), 1982 Paris Marathon (allegedly 3:20).*

CHAPTER 5

RUNNING CLUBS

*We are runners when we lace up our trainers, come
rain or shine, early flight or late-night deadline.*

SAM MURPHY, COACH

A gentleman's club?

Running in the nineteenth and early
twentieth century in Britain was divided
between the professionals, who were
often in low-paid employment, and
the wealthy who joined exclusive
'gentleman amateur' clubs, such as
the Thames Hare & Hounds where
tradesmen were not welcomed. Still in
existence to this day, the club remained

a very conservative institution not allowing women to enter until
1981, the year of the first London Marathon and the Great North Run.

The British running boom in the 1980s saw clubs like London-
based Serpentine created in response to the new breed of runners
and a slew of races being created. The club was established by

runners training for that year's London Marathon. It now boasts over 2,100 members with around 42 per cent women, and membership from all corners of the globe and walks of life.

The archaic, outdated values of the early clubs have long ago disappeared and been replaced with clubs seeking to meet the needs of all runners, no matter their gender, age or ability.

A common misconception is that running clubs are full of virile, testosterone-fuelled young alpha males and females, with lithe bodies and egos to match. A casual observation of any local 10 k race would make it obvious that running clubs have a cross-section of membership of all abilities. Running clubs can be found in every part of the UK, some catering for specific sections of society. Northern Frontrunners are a lesbian, gay, bisexual and transgender running club; Vegan Runners UK and Christian Runners both have an obvious membership base and Fetch Everyone is an Internet-based club. It's the shared love of running which unites all clubs and their members.

Why join a club?

The benefits of joining a running club are many, including the following:

A great place to meet other runners

They cater for all abilities

Local running knowledge, such as routes and good physios

Designated and structured training plans

Support, encouragement and motivation

Runners with shared aims

Social activities, including trips to races and obligatory post-race celebratory meals

Width of knowledge and experience amongst members

Reduced race entry fees

Whilst it is not necessary to be a club member to be a runner, a new joiner might also experience a psychological shift in their perceptions of themselves. They may no longer see themselves as someone who runs. Instead, they are a runner; a small but important change, which can lead to self-belief, confidence and willingness to try something new.

Fetch Everyone

This Internet-based club records over 17,000 registered users on its website. The site provides a free service allowing runners to record what they are doing, interact with other users and complete training diaries. An extensive forum page promotes lively chat and discussion about all manner of things, not always running related. Its members are called 'Fetchies' and wear eye-catching colourful club gear, which makes them stand out at races and helps them to identify each other.

> *Fetch member Naomi Prasad was the first UK woman to run 100 marathons before the age of 30. She married fellow Fetchie Mark Studdart in 2012 having met through the site. Prasad also briefly held the title of the UK's fastest female marathon runner of the decade, with a time of 4:18:49, which she ran in Zurich on New Year's Day 2010. Unfortunately, she only held the title for three weeks until her time was bettered.*

The Bob Graham 24 Hour Club

Membership of the Bob Graham 24 Hour Club is prized in fell-running circles. The club is open to anyone who can complete the 72-mile Bob Graham Round in less than 24 hours. Set in the Lake District, the route is named after a Keswick guesthouse owner who set the record for the quickest time in 1932, although it was broken in 1960 by Alan Heaton. Sound easy? Factor in that the precise route covers 42 peaks, 27,000 feet of ascent and descent, and peaks including Skiddaw (3,054 ft), Bowfell (2,960 ft) and Scafell Pike (3,206 ft), and it's little wonder membership is so precious.

The club opened its tent flaps to potential peak baggers in 1960. Twenty years later, the task was so difficult membership stood at only 141. By the end of 2012, that had grown to 1,781 hardy men and women, helped by the growth of knowledge within the club of the best routes. Over the years, there have been remarkable achievements: Roger Baumeister running the round twice in 46:34:30 in 1979; Billy Bland's unfeasibly quick 13:53:00 in 1982; Nicky Spinks' 18:12:00 women's record in 2012; and the winter rounds (most are in the height of summer), when light is limited and the terrain more difficult. The small band that has extended the number of peaks bagged in the same time limit are in another league. Mark Hartell's 77-peak run in 1997 in 23:47 is worthy of a chapter on its own. Any prospective member would benefit from reading Richard Askwith's *Feet in the Clouds* – and then do something simpler, like run a marathon carrying a fridge. Yep, that's been done – and it's easier.

The 100 Marathon Club

This is slightly more difficult to join as the UK club requires runners to have completed 100 officially measured and verifiable road or trail marathons. There are 100 Clubs all over the world, including New Zealand, Finland and Germany, some of which will allow training runs to count towards a runner's total. The stats of some of the UK club members are very impressive and include the following records (as at April 2013):

100 Club records (UK)

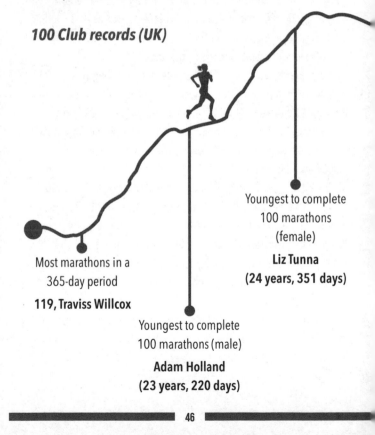

Most marathons in a
365-day period
119, Traviss Willcox

Youngest to complete
100 marathons (male)
**Adam Holland
(23 years, 220 days)**

Youngest to complete
100 marathons
(female)
**Liz Tunna
(24 years, 351 days)**

Quickest 0 to 100
marathons
**688 days,
Traviss Willcox**

Quickest time to
complete any 50
marathons

**114 days,
Traviss Willcox**

Quickest time to
complete any 100
marathons

**284 days,
Traviss Willcox**

100 Club records (UK) continued...

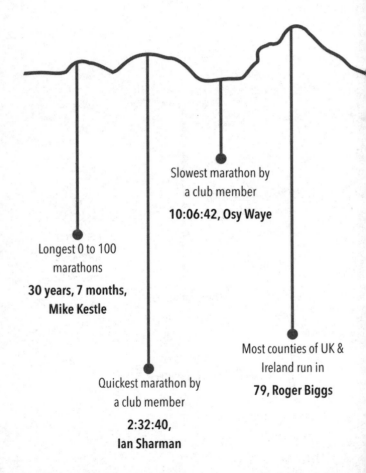

Slowest marathon by
a club member

10:06:42, Osy Waye

Longest 0 to 100
marathons

**30 years, 7 months,
Mike Kestle**

Most counties of UK &
Ireland run in

79, Roger Biggs

Quickest marathon by
a club member

**2:32:40,
Ian Sharman**

Most USA states
(including
Washington DC)
run in

51, Roger Biggs

Most wine-drinking
marathons

16, Jean-Loup Taisne

Most continents run
on in the same year

7, Roger Biggs

Tony Phoenix-Morrison (aka Tony the Fridge) ran Kielder Marathon with a 40-kg fridge strapped to his back, a month after running the course of the Great North Run on 30 consecutive days, including the main race. In April 2013, he also carried a 42-kg Smeg fridge around Newcastle quayside for a full 24 hours on a solo run to raise funds for the Sir Bobby Robson Foundation.

Carpe viam

Despite its alarming name, the Dead Runners Society doesn't require death as a qualifying joining requirement, although once in, members are 'deads'. The DRS is a worldwide virtual online running club founded by Chris Conn in Texas in 1991, merging the power of emails and later the Internet with sport. The aim of the club is to informally share anything running related, from meditation to marathons. It has its own flag (incorporating a running figure and smiley emoticon), race wear, terminology, annual world conferences and offshoots of the main body around the world including STiLldeads (St Louis Dead Runners Society), SOBER Deads (Southern Ontario and Buffalo Expired Runners) and DEADeNZ (Dead Runners New Zealand). Primarily a running community, discussion pages extend to music, parenting and the other dark art, triathlons.

The Ever Presents

This is a club that many marathoners would like to enter, although it's impossible to do so for any amount of money and, with the passage of time, its membership is shrinking. The Ever Present club comprises 15 runners who, as of 2013, have run every London Marathon since the first race in 1981. Over the years membership has declined and, at their own admission, they 'have less hair, less teeth, less ability – however their force, dedication and perseverance is still there'. Given Chris Finill clocked a very impressive 2:50:32 in 2012, the 'less ability' statement is debatable.

> *Chris Finill obtained the Guinness World Record for running the most consecutive editions of the World Marathon Majors in under 3:30, between 29 March 1981 and 25 April 2010.*

Should I join a club?

The answer is, well, it's up to you. Olympian Lorraine Moller said, 'For me, running is a lifestyle and an art. I'm far more interested in the magic of it than the mechanics'. There will be runners who are happy to do their own thing and those that would benefit from other runners around them. The key is to find the magic, no matter how you get there (as long as it's not on a bike).

CHAPTER 6

INSPIRATIONAL RUNNERS

We can't all be heroes because somebody has to sit on the curb and clap as they go by.

WILL ROGERS, US HUMOURIST

James Cleveland Owens *(AKA Jesse Owens)*
(12 September 1913 - 31 March 1980)
Nickname: The Buckeye Bullet

Find the good. It's all around you. Find it, showcase it and you'll start believing it.

JESSE OWENS, ATHLETE

Born in Oakville, Alabama, during the First World War, Owens was an African-American who took part in a race widely regarded as the greatest of all time, winning gold in the 100 m final at the Berlin Olympics on 3 August 1936. That medal, along with three further golds won in the 200 m, the long jump and the 100 m relay in the same games, remain an evocative symbol of one man's triumph over the fascism of Nazi Germany and its abhorrent racial ideals of an Aryan super race that 'would last for 1,000 years'. The summer games were designed to promote the ideals of Nazism and give Hitler's rhetoric and the Third Reich's propaganda a world platform. Guy Walters records in *Berlin Games: How Hitler Stole the Olympic Dream* that the Führer's Minister of Propaganda Joseph Goebbels wrote in his diary, 'white humanity should be ashamed of itself', after three African-Americans won gold medals during one day of the games. Depite their achievements, it is Owens who was the star of the show with his gold medal haul.

The political significance of Owen's wins, and those of his contemporaries such as Cornelius Johnson in the high jump, shouldn't overshadow the track achievements of an athlete who has been described as 'perfection personified'. Prior to the games, he broke world records for the long jump, low hurdles and various sprint distances. In Berlin he ran 10.3 seconds in the first round of the 100 m, 10.2 in the second round for new world and Olympic records, subsequently disallowed due to the tail wind, 10.4 in the semi and 10.3 in the final, when the wind was also too strong. The German Erich Borchmeyer (who Owens had beaten in a 100 yards race in Los Angeles Memorial Coliseum in 1932) trailed in second from last.

On 4 August, he set a new games record of 21.1 in the 200 m heats and bettered that in the final with 20.7. He didn't dominate the long jump, almost going out in the first round, eventually beating another German into second place with leaps of 7.94 m and 8.06 m. On 8 August, he helped the relay team to a new world record in the 4 x 100 m. His achievements would not be repeated until Carl Lewis' performance in the 1984 Olympics in Los Angeles.

Owens left a lasting legacy that continues to inspire beyond the confines of sporting success.

Grete Waitz
(1 October 1953 – 19 April 2011)
Nickname: Grandma

*When I came to New York in 1978, I was a full-time school
teacher and track runner, and determined to retire from
competitive running. But winning the New York City
Marathon kept me running for another decade.*

GRETE WAITZ, ATHLETE

Winning the New York City Marathon certainly changed Norwegian
Grete Waitz from a good track runner into the world's best female
marathon runner of her era. In her youth, Waitz set European junior
records – although her senior career was mixed with significant
success and failure on the track, failing to make two Olympic finals in
the 1970s. In 1978, she was invited to run by New York City Marathon
race director and founder Fred Lebow. Almost by accident, she found
her most successful race distance. On her marathon debut, she ran
a world record time of 2:32:29, reducing it in 1979 to 2:27:33 and
2:25:41 in 1980. She would eventually win the race nine times,
lowering the world record in London in 1983 to 2:25:29 and winning
gold at the Helsinki World Championships that year. In 1984 she won
silver at the inaugural women's Olympic marathon. She won London
again in 1986 and Stockholm in 1988, but was forced to retire from
the 1988 games with a knee injury. In 1992, she ran New York City
with the terminally ill Lebow, who passed away two years later.

She also won many shorter road and cross-country events including the famous Falmouth Road Race. She decimated the course record at the Great North Run in 1984 with a time of 1:10:27 and she also medalled at the World Cross Country Championships seven times. Her achievements at a time when marathon running for the masses was growing led the way for women in particular to enter races of that length, building on the inspiration of Bobbi Gibb who without a race number unofficially finished the Boston Marathon in 1966 and Kathy Switzer, the first official female finisher, a year later. Waitz transcended gender stereotypes and will forever remain an icon to male and female runners alike.

Steve Roland Prefontaine
(25 January 1951 – 30 May 1975)
Nickname: Pre

A lot of people run a race to see who is fastest.
I run to see who has the most guts.

STEVE PREFONTAINE, ATHLETE

Born in Coos Bay, Oregon, 'Pre' was a cross-country and track school and college runner who rose to international stardom before his death in a car crash at the age of just 24, setting a host of records at distances ranging between 2,000–10,000 m. Whilst at the University of Oregon he won multiple NCAA (National Collegiate Athletic Association) titles, setting nine collegiate track records in the process. In 1970, he made the cover of *Sports Illustrated* and in 1972, at the age of 21, he finished fourth in the Olympic 5,000 m in a time of 13:28.2, behind Lasse Virén (13:26.4), Mohammed Gammoudi (13:27.4) and Ian Stewart (13:27.6). He brought athletics to a wider audience in America along with runners including Frank Shorter, who arguably were the catalyst for the running boom of the 1970s. At the time of his death, Pre held every American record between 2,000 and 10,000 m.

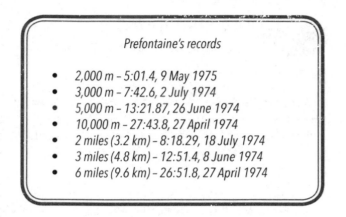

Prefontaine's records

- *2,000 m – 5:01.4, 9 May 1975*
- *3,000 m – 7:42.6, 2 July 1974*
- *5,000 m – 13:21.87, 26 June 1974*
- *10,000 m – 27:43.8, 27 April 1974*
- *2 miles (3.2 km) – 8:18.29, 18 July 1974*
- *3 miles (4.8 km) – 12:51.4, 8 June 1974*
- *6 miles (9.6 km) – 26:51.8, 27 April 1974*

The loss of such a talent sent shockwaves around the world and yet his legacy lives on. At the rock where his life ended, a memorial reads, 'For your dedication and loyalty, To your principles and beliefs... For your love, warmth, and friendship. For your family and friends... You are missed by so many and you will never be forgotten...' And he's not. Since 1975, an international track event called the Prefontaine Classic has been held in Eugene, Oregon, and the 10 k Prefontaine Memorial Run takes place each September in Coos Bay. For a runner there can be no better tribute than a race being held in your honour.

Kathrine Switzer
(born 5 January 1947)
Nickname: The Marathon Woman

When I go to the Boston Marathon now, I have wet shoulders – women fall into my arms crying. They're weeping for joy because running has changed their lives. They feel they can do anything.

KATHRINE SWITZER, RUNNER AND AUTHOR

The first Boston Marathon took place in 1897, with just 15 male runners. It was a bastion of prejudice and women were not allowed to enter. In 1967, using just her initials, Kathrine Switzer was able to secure a number and ran with her coach Arnie Briggs and boyfriend, Tom Miller. Four miles into the race an official, Jock Semple, lunged and tried to snatch her number screaming 'get the hell out of my race' in full view of the watching media truck which had been following from early on. A swift shove from Miller sent him flying and changed the course of athletics history. Eventually finishing in approximately 4:20, the event transformed her into a prominent figurehead in the fight to allow women to compete in long-distance races.

To put the prejudices of the day into perspective, no woman had been allowed to run the Olympic marathon despite two turning up to do so at the inaugural 1896 modern Olympic Games. That wouldn't change until 1984. A British woman, Violet Percy, was timed in a marathon officially at 3:40:22 in 1926, which stood as a world best until 1960 as women were not allowed to enter races. Even the women's 800 m was cancelled after the 1928 games until 1960, over fears it was too much for them.

Switzer became a champion of the right for women to enter races and campaigned tirelessly for an Olympic women's marathon. In 1972, Boston finally opened its doors to all. In athletic terms, Switzer was an accomplished runner, winning the New York City Marathon in 3:07:29 in 1973 (with times of 3:16:02 and 3:02:57 in the straddling years) and with a personal best of 2:51:37 at the Boston Marathon in 1975, which most marathon runners would give their teeth for. She was named Female Runner of the Decade by *Runner's World*, became an author, and continues to inspire men and women alike.

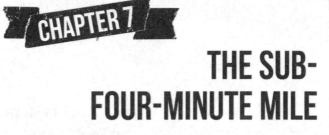

CHAPTER 7

THE SUB-FOUR-MINUTE MILE

*Whether we athletes liked it or not, the four-minute mile had
become rather like an Everest; a challenge to the human spirit,
it was a barrier that seemed to defy all attempts to break it,
an irksome reminder that men's striving might be in vain.*

ROGER BANNISTER, ATHLETE

The history

Attempts to run a mile in a time faster than four minutes captured the
public's imagination long before the feat was finally achieved on 6 May
1954 at Iffley Road, Oxford, by Roger Bannister in a time of 3:59.40. By
the 1700s in Britain and further afield, gambling on races of differing
distances, including the mile, was widespread, with reports appearing in
publications such as *The Sporting Magazine* of large wagers being placed.
One of the first athletics books, *Pedestrianism*, recounts an attempt at
the start of the nineteenth century to run a measured street mile – and
whilst the reported time of 4:10 is impressive, it is impossible to confirm.
With the sums involved and the incentives to manipulate these events,
reliance can't be placed on the accuracy of records of the day.

> *The 'metric mile' in race terms is the 1,500 m and is commonly run by professional athletes on a track. It is 19 yards 21 inches short of a Roman mile, which was 1,000 Roman strides, a stride being two paces.*

The pros vs amateurs

The growth of professional promoters and runners aided the cause of breaking the four-minute mile barrier, as it led to athletes with training regimes whose sole purpose was to make money, and to races taking place on enclosed tracks, which the public had to pay to enter. These could be more accurately measured and timed, using systems that had been developed for horse racing. Ironically, in the years that followed the creation of the AAA, the conflict between professionals and amateurs hindered the four-minute barrier being broken. The organisation imposed a strict code seeking to ensure that the custodians of the sport as they saw it – the gentlemen amateurs who ran for pleasure rather than financial gain – were the only ones whose records counted. The amateurs were by their nature part-time athletes who did not train to the standard needed to break the barrier.

A verifiable benchmark of 4:12.75 was set in an accurate, timed race by professional Walter George in 1886, a record which stood for 29 years until it was edged by Norman Taber in 1915 with 4:12.6. George's time was not recognised by the amateur authorities, who still hold American John Paul Jones' time of 4:14.4 set in 1913 as the first world record.

It is difficult to pinpoint the moment the potential for breaking the barrier became a realistic objective. Did runners at the turn of the nineteenth century truly believe it would happen? Certainly many coaches of the era didn't and the longer George's record stood, the further away the prospect seemed.

The modern comparison is the sub-two-hour marathon barrier. It seems such an impossible task and yet since Spyridon Louis' marathon time of 2:58:50 in the 1896 Olympics, the world record has dropped by over 55 minutes to 2:03:38. Will future generations wonder why it took so long to be broken? It is the sense of anticipation that makes the sub-two-hour potential as exciting as the sub-four-minute mile was in the 1950s.

A matter of time

In the years that followed George and Taber, runners including Paavo Nurmi in the 1920s and Jack Lovelock in the 1930s reduced the world record. Glenn Cunningham ran the mile in 4:04.4 on an indoor, wind-free track, which was therefore not recognised as a record. Nevertheless, it suggested that the barrier could be broken.

By the 1940s, Gunder Hägg and Arne Andersson had equaled or lowered the record six times, with the former recording 4:01.4 in 1945. It had taken 59 years to shave just over 11 seconds off George's time, but it was so close, the sense of excitement at the prospect touched athletes and the public all over the globe thanks to increasingly sophisticated means of communication. The following eight years and 293 days following Hägg's record were one of the most exciting periods ever in the mile's history, as runners such as Bannister, Wes Santee and John Landy tried to break the barrier time and time again.

Mile benchmark times before Bannister

1886 Walter George **4:12.75**
1913 John Paul Jones (IAAF 1st WR) **4:14.4**
1915 Norman Taber **4:12.6**
1923 Paavo Nurmi **4:10.4**
1931 Jules Ladoumègue **4:09.2**
1933 Jack Lovelock **4:07.6**
1934 Glenn Cunningham **4:06.8**
1937 Sydney Wooderson **4:06.4**
1942 Gunder Hägg **4:06.2**
1942 Arne Andersson **4:06.2**
1942 Gunder Hägg **4:04.6**
1943 Arne Andersson **4:02.6**
1944 Arne Andersson **4:01.6**
1945 Gunder Hägg **4:01.4**

The Race

Bannister was an Oxford medical student and part-time athlete, who adopted a professional approach to the mile attempt, following his failure to win a medal at the previous Olympic Games. Pacers were strictly not allowed in the 1950s, which is why his running mates on the day, Chris Chataway and Chris Brasher, had to be seen to be trying to run the race as well as they could. The reality is that the three friends had trained meticulously together working out the pace needed for each lap. The race was broadcast live on BBC Radio and commentated by the 1924 Olympic medalist Harold Abrahams. The organised and rehearsed race plan came together as they hit each lap target, until Bannister crossed the line and ran into the history books. 'In the last fifty yards my body had long since exhausted its energy but it went on running just the same', said Bannister, who admitted that it was Chataway and Brasher who got him there.

Oh so close

Wes Santee ran 4:01.4 just 23 days after Bannister's record, equaling Hägg's 1945 world record; shortly afterwards in another race he recorded a time of 4:00.6. On 21 June 1954, John Landy became 'the Buzz Aldrin and Sherpa Tenzing of the athletics world', recording a mile time in 3:57.9 (rounded up to 3:58), shattering Bannister's record that had lasted a mere 46 days.

> *In the 'Race of the Century' at the British Empire and Commonwealth Games in Vancouver, British Columbia, on the 7 August 1954, Bannister and Landy became the first men in history to record a time lower than four minutes in the same race; Bannister edged it in 3:58.8 with Landy finishing in 3:59.6*

By 1957, Herb Elliot reduced the record to 3:54.5 and in the years that followed the record fell still further, although the 3:50 barrier resisted strongly. It was not until 1975 that John Walker, of New Zealand, ran 3:49.4. The current list of the ten fastest mile times ever run is dominated by Morocco's Hicham El Guerrouj, who appears an astonishing seven times. His 1999 world record benchmark of 3:43.13 stands supreme.

Why is it special?

Bannister's run has stood the test of time as one of the landmark achievements in history, and not just athletics. After the barrier had been broken, he compared it with climbing Everest for the first time. The first person to climb Everest? Hilary. First on the moon? Armstrong. First to run a four-minute mile? Actually, it was Derek Ibbotson, who ran an exact 240 seconds on 3 September 1957. Due to a nanosecond, however, it's the now-famous medical student's achievement that will forever be linked with the mile.

> *The record for the fastest one-mile sack race is 16:41, set on 19 May 2007 by Ashrita Furman (USA) in Baruun Salaa in Mongolia.*

Anyone who has ever attempted to run a fast mile knows one thing – it hurts. A miler has to have the perfect combination of strength, speed and endurance. For the sprinters it's over all too quickly. For the 5,000 m or longer, races are run at a patient, planned pace, with breaks for the line in the latter stages. The mile requires intense effort from the gun, with each compelling lap tightening the grip on the observer. 'Almost every part of the mile is tactically important; you can never let down, never stop thinking and you can be beaten at almost any point. I suppose you could say it's like life', said Landy. The pain is etched in the faces of athletes on the home straight. Knowing they have pushed their bodies to near total physical exertion and their minds to their threshold is inspirational.

World track records for the mile – women

Time	Name	Nationality	Race location	Date
4:12.56	Svetlana Masterkova	Russia	Zurich	14 August 1996
4:15.61	Paula Ivan	Romania	Nice	10 July 1989
4:15.8	Natalya Artyomova	Russia	Leningrad	5 August 1984
4:16.71	Mary Slaney	USA	Zurich	21 August 1985
4:17.00	Natalya Artyomova	Russia	Barcelona	20 September 1991
4:17.25	Sonia O'Sullivan	Ireland	Oslo	22 July 1994
4:17.33	Maricica Puică	Romania	Zurich	21 August 1985
4:17.44	Maricica Puică	Romania	Rieti	16 September 1982
4:17.57	Zola Pieterse	Great Britain	Zurich	21 August 1985
4:17.75	Maryam Yusuf Jamal	Bahrain	Brussels	14 September 2007

World track records for the mile – men

Time	Name	Nationality	Race location	Date
3:43.13	Hicham El Guerrouj	Morocco	Rome	7 July 1999
3:43.40	Noah Ngeny	Kenya	Rome	7 July 1999
3:44.39	Noureddine Morceli	Algeria	Rieti	5 September 1993
3:44.60	Hicham El Guerrouj	Morocco	Nice	16 July 1998
3:44.90	Hicham El Guerrouj	Morocco	Oslo	4 July 1997
3:44.95	Hicham El Guerrouj	Morocco	Rome	29 June 2001
3:45.19	Noureddine Morceli	Algeria	Zurich	16 August 1995
3:45.64	Hicham El Guerrouj	Morocco	Berlin	26 August 1997
3:45.96	Hicham El Guerrouj	Morocco	London	5 August 2000
3:46.24	Hicham El Guerrouj	Morocco	Oslo	28 July 2000

Just for the pros?

Well, no. Whilst mile races are not so frequently staged as races of other distances, they are out there.

The Queen Street Golden Mile in Auckland, New Zealand, was first run in 1972 and was won by Tony Polhill in 3:47.6, beating the then track world record of 3:51.1, held by Jim Ryun of the USA. In 1982, Steve Scott's winning time of 3:31.25 was 16 seconds quicker than Seb Coe's track world record of 3:47.33. In 1983, the *Guinness Book of Records'* world's fastest mile was recorded in the race, as Mike Boit of Kenya ran in 3:28.36, which still eclipses Hicham El Guerrouj's track record. Christine Hughes won the women's event in 1983 in 4:02.93, which still beats the track record of 4:12.56 set by Svetlana Masterkova in 1996. The reason for such fast times? The race is run on a ridiculously steep downhill street. In 2013, the organisers allowed a small number of non-professional athletes to enter, with parachutes, soundness of mind and first-aid experience being optional.

The other way

Hills aren't always a guarantee for a quick time. In 2012, the first runner home in the Ilkley mile race took an apparently leisurely 7:29, whilst last place was 17:22. The fact that it was all uphill might have had something to do with it.

The Antarctic mile

Set up alongside the Antarctic Ice Marathon, this little fun run a few hundred miles from the South Pole is a tad chilly and isolated. The entry fee of €10,500 and five days in the Antarctic makes the Ilkley race seem a little more accessible.

CHEATERS AND RULE BENDERS

*Each of us has been put on earth with the ability to
do something well. We cheat ourselves and the world
if we don't use that ability as best we can.*

GEORGE ALLEN SR, US SENATOR AND LAWYER

Cheaters never prosper

It is a sad fact that in professional sport, there will always be people
who will try to gain an unfair advantage over their rivals. Athletics isn't
immune to the use of performance-enhancing drugs. Before the fall
of the Berlin Wall, almost no East German athlete tested positive for
banned drugs. Afterwards, they were queuing around the shattered
remains of the wall to complain about the strange substances they
had been told to ingest by a state-controlled doping policy, which
forced the German government to put aside a large compensation
fund to meet claims by 193 athletes.

Who can forget the eye-popping, vein-bulging Canadian sprinter
Ben Johnson on the start line of the 1988 100 m Olympic final in

Seoul, South Korea? Having initially won gold, he was stripped two days later of the medal and two world records after testing positive for a banned substance. Judging by his appearance in the race, it would have been odd if he hadn't been using something. Four years earlier, Martti Vainio's 10,000 m silver was quashed for drug misuse. The once great American sprint queen Marion Jones admitted using banned drugs, was stripped of her five Olympic medals and went to jail for lying to the authorities. Closer to home, Dwain Chambers received a two-year ban for taking an illegal substance, although he was subsequently integrated back into the sport, a decision not met with universal approval. Athletics does not have a cheat on the scale of cycling's Lance Armstrong but it needs to be vigilant in all areas and make sure its pros remain clean.

Well-known rule breakers

There is no drug-testing policy for the thousands of runners who turn out every weekend for races, with much less incentive to take anything in the first place. It isn't worth risking your health to come 211th instead of 452nd in a race. There have been runners who have tried to cheat in other ways, both pros and amateurs. In 2009, the Chicago Marathon disqualified 252 runners who missed two or more timing mats, while a year later the New York City Marathon knocked out 71, with at least 46 believed to have not gone the distance. In 2011, one competitor in the Montreal Marathon was disqualified after being caught jumping on a push-bike to make up time.

Fred Lorz

In the 1904 St Louis Marathon, Lorz represented the USA in a race beset by heat, dusty roads and poor organisation. At the 9-mile mark he dropped out and was given a lift by his manager for the next 11 miles until his car broke down. He jumped out and ran the rest, crossing the finish line in first place in front of the probably half-drunk Thomas Hicks. The truth eventually came out, after which he claimed that it was a practical joke. He was banned for life by the AAA, but it was subsequently rescinded. He would go on to win the Boston Marathon in 1905, in a time considerably quicker than Hicks' gold-medal performance and the existing Olympic record of Spyridon Louis. (This race also featured Cuban postman Felix Carbajal, who stopped to eat rotten apples in an orchard, experienced stomach pain, had to lie down and still finished fourth in his adapted street clothes.)

Rosie Ruiz

The most famous amateur cheat has to be Rosie Ruiz, who came first in the 1980 Boston Marathon in a course record time of 2:31:56. Her lack of sweat-drenched clothes and the facts that she didn't know what 'splits' were and the second-placed woman hadn't seen her throughout the race raised suspicion. When two witnesses said she had appeared out of the crowd with half a mile to go, the game was up and the win was awarded to Jacqueline Gareau. Later, a photographer also said she had seen Ruiz on the subway during the New York City Marathon in 1979, a race she had used to gain entry to Boston. Despite the weight of evidence against her, she never admitted to cheating.

Abbes Tehami

Algerian runner Abbes Tehami lost the Brussels Marathon in 1991 by a matter of millimetres. Having apparently started the race with a moustache, he finished clean-shaven. Even given his apparent prowess at distance running, that would have been an impressive stunt to pull off. It transpired that his hairy-lipped coach had run the first 7 miles (11 km) or so, before swapping with his clean-shaven protégé intent on claiming the prize money of more than $7,000.

The Motsoeneng Brothers

Whilst not identical twins, Sergio and Fika Motsoeneng swapped places and clothes in a mobile toilet during the 1999 Comrades 56-mile ultra marathon in South Africa between Durban and Pietermaritzburg. They were later caught after a newspaper published a photo of them wearing watches on opposite wrists. Perhaps the most humiliating part is that, despite their antics, they only came ninth. In 2010, Sergio returned to claim third place, only to have his medal stripped and winnings cancelled for using a banned substance.

Roberto Madrazo

Roberto Madrazo was a Mexican presidential hopeful who ran the 2007 Berlin Marathon in a time of 2:41:12, good enough to put him into the elite category. His finish photo shows him arms aloft, crossing the line smiling in a hat, pants and baggy running jacket, barely sweating. The runners around him are in vests, shorts and are on their last legs, as would be expected with such a fast finishing time. It transpired he missed two timing mats, which on the Berlin course are just impossible to avoid and 'ran' 9 miles (14.5 km) in 21 minutes.

Chinese students

At the 2010 Xiamen Marathon in China, an unusually high number of students from a particular school in the Shandong province clocked remarkably quick finishing times. A high percentage even seemed to cross the finishing line at the same time, frequently three abreast. The answer? A large number had given their timing chips to faster students who would carry two or three at a time, or others hitched lifts in order to try to get a time below 2:34, which would give them extra points for coveted university places.

Rob Sloan

The Kielder Marathon in Northumbria has a strong claim to Britain's most beautiful run, as its website claims, adjacent to a huge reservoir. It's also tough, on undulating forest paths with the last 6 miles (9.5 km) taking in some leg-sapping climbs. Perhaps that's why former Sunderland Harrier runner Sloan jumped on one of the shuttle buses waiting at the 20-mile point, hopped off near the end and proceeded to run in for third place. After the real third-place finisher complained he had only seen two runners in front of him, Rob was eventually disqualified whilst still protesting his innocence. He had won a 10 k race the day before in a legitimate time of 38:10. Who runs that fast or far the day before a marathon? No wonder he dropped out. At least the organiser, Olympian Steve Cram, had the last laugh, as the website now describes the race as 'tranquil, challenging, rewarding... but no bus ride'.

Is it worth it?

Whatever the length of the race, the satisfaction is in finishing regardless of time or position. The person who crosses the line in last place has covered the same distance as the winner and will be applauded by their fellow competitors. It takes a special kind of determination to be out there for six-plus hours with 8 miles to go, knowing that half the field will already be on the way home and tucking into something hearty. George Sheehan said, 'It's very hard in the beginning to understand that the whole idea is not to beat the other runners. Eventually you learn that competition is against the little voice inside you that wants you to quit.' The majority of runners never step on a podium, bank a winner's cheque or take part for any reason other than they want to do the best they can. Taking a shortcut or swapping places just doesn't make any sense and deprives the runner of the thing that matters the most: the sense of achievement.

CHAPTER 9

TYPES OF RUNNING RACES

I always loved running… it was something you could do by yourself, and under your own power. You could go in any direction, fast or slow as you wanted, fighting the wind if you felt like it, seeking out new sights just on the strength of your feet and the courage of your lungs.

JESSE OWENS, ATHLETE

Adventure vs trail vs road

The runner has an abundance of options to choose from, in terms of distance, terrain, adventure, navigation and more. Most will start their careers on the road and might work towards an accessible 5 k at a local parkrun. As fitness, confidence and aspirations grow, runs will increase in length and thoughts will turn towards 10 k races and longer. For many, the certainty of the road is enough; it provides easily measurable distances, an even surface and repeatable routes over which progress can be charted.

New runners tend to focus on time and distance improvements. Whilst that satisfaction remains, with experience they will start to look further afield for different challenges. The world of trail or fell running, self-navigating mountain races, orienteering events, mixed-terrain team relay events, adventure and obstacle runs might open up new and exciting chapters. For the speed merchants, the 400 m oval track might be their calling. Some will integrate the dark arts of cycling and swimming in triathlon races, although runners argue that their sport is the hardest, as it doesn't involve sitting down or having a splash at the local pool. The Brownlee brothers may disagree.

Lucio Fregona won the Fregona Marathon in Italy in 2004 and Helen Clitheroe won the Clitheroe 10 k in England in the same year.

Which race to choose?

There is a burgeoning list of races fighting for the runner's pound every weekend, from 5 k races to marathons and beyond. Organisers have to think of ever-more ingenious ways to entice people to their shindigs, frequently starting with the race name. No longer is it enough to call your race the West Lothian 5 k. Titles such as the Snakes Pit Challenge or The Pain Barrier seek to grab the attention and wallets of weekend athletes, implying the event is tougher than the rest. Why else would it be called 'The Ball Breaker' or some other similarly testosterone-charged handle? In recent years, a fancy title hasn't been enough as discerning athletes have cottoned on to the fact that despite the name, it is after all just another 5 k or 10 k race.

Smaller events can offer good value for money with lower entry fees, as can races without a large goody bag. Many running clubs put on races for the benefit of their fellow runners in other clubs, who return the favour by putting on their own events. Inevitably, club events tend to be cheaper than those put on by organisations intending to make a profit. Avoid being seduced by the title, pick a distance and/or terrain and decide what you want to achieve. If you want a new personal best, stick to the tarmac. If you want to feel at one with nature and forget personal best hunting, hit the trails. If you thrive on exhaustion and don't mind risking injury, try adventure or obstacle races. Whatever the time, distance or ground you choose, remember one thing – you are not just out there jogging. You have become a racer.

Road and track running

Most athletes will train and race on tarmac at some point or other, more of which later. While a 400 m oval track is not the preserve of professional athletes, amateur

races are rare. There are running clubs throughout the UK which have excellent track facilities, like Biggleswade AC and Inverness Harriers. Some host open track meetings, which tend to attract club athletes to programmes replicating the main shorter Olympic distances. There are notable exceptions such as the Crawley 12-hour Track Race, which in 2013 saw 1st-placed veteran John McBurney run 71 miles 370 yards (115 km). The Melbourne Tan Track 100 km Ultra takes place in Australia, whilst the Self-Transcendence Ultra track race in Ottawa, Canada, describes itself as 'the longest-running 24-hour race in the world'. In 2012, Greek athlete Yiannis Kouros ran 218.9 km (136.018 miles) on an indoor 400 m track. Track running isn't the preserve of professionals and, with a bit of research, events of any distance can be found up and down the country and further afield for those who want to pull on their running spikes.

Adventure/obstacle racing

A typical adventure race will involve two or more endurance disciplines combining foot, pedal or waterpower, and are frequently self-navigating in  remote areas. They range from two or three-hour sprint races to multi-day events for soloists or teams; the Adidas Terrex Swift is a two-day non-stop event for mixed-sex teams of four, incorporating trail running, mountain biking and kayaking.

At the extreme end of the scale is the ten-day Chilean Patagonia Expedition Race, known as the Race to the End of the World as it heads 565 km (351 miles) towards Antarctica. The route changes every year and attracts an international field, which has included athletes from the UK, Russia, Mexico, Sweden and Kazakhstan. Its aim is to raise global awareness of the fragile, diverse and threatened environment in which it takes place, while at the same time seeking to bring sustainable tourism to the area.

*I don't measure a man's success by how high he climbs
but how high he bounces when he hits bottom.*

GEORGE PATTON, US ARMY GENERAL

Obstacle races were primarily imported from the USA in the early 1990s and blend running with all manner of weird and wonderful impediments in races of varying times and distances. The noughties witnessed a rapid increase in obstacle races in the UK jumping onto the already existing bandwagon of famously difficult challenge events, such as the Grizzly Run in the Devon village of Seaton, which has taken place annually since 1988 and relies on good old-fashioned sand, hills and shingle beaches to dish out punishment to its competitors. Events organised by companies such as Rat Race or Tough Mudder throw in all manner of obstacles along the way. They also follow the unwritten rule that the harder the race, the more extreme the title needs to be, implying that the combatants will be faced with life-threatening experiences, momentous hurdles and almost insuperable challenges. The Spartan Beast or Tough Guy claim to be the hardest events in the world, and tell the competitor that if they finish, not only will they have entered the lion's den, but they will have looked in its mouth and flossed its teeth.

It's unlikely that a 12 k or 20-mile cross-country affair, which combines running, mudbaths, fire, rivers, cycling, straw bales, kayaking and 10,000 volts of electricity to negotiate will make it to the Olympics. That's not going to deter the Indiana Jones types who find it impossible to readjust to a standard running race. Once they have crossed the threshold, it's hard to come back. The public's desire for something different to road racing has underpinned the popularity and continued growth of these races in recent years and their tamer cousins – exercise boot camps. At a basic level, these types of events share the same intrinsic physical and psychological skills needed by anyone who takes part, as aerobic fitness and body strength combine with mental toughness.

Trail, fell and mountain running

It's tempting to think that when astronaut Neil Armstrong said 'I believe that the Good Lord gave us a finite number of heartbeats  and I'm damned if I'm going to use up mine running up and down a street', he was actually promoting the benefits of trail, fell or mountain running. Hewn from the same tree, all are off-road on natural terrain, frequently involve self-navigation and those that undertake them generally don't do it for quick times, as trail marathons tend to take longer than their road equivalents.

Trail running is accessible even for committed urbanites. Britain has many long-distance paths running all over the country, such as the 1,400 km All Wales Coast Path, the 160 km South Downs Way – which hosts many good running events on its tough, undulating trails – the 176 km Cleveland Way or the 80 km Moray Coast Trail in Scotland. The country is crossed with local paths and trails offering runners the chance to escape the hardness of the pavement. It provides softer ground – which helps with injury prevention – and lets runners see things they might not otherwise.

The sight of a nesting osprey searching for food for its chicks just off a woodland trail in the middle of Scotland; the views from Snowdon; being stuck knee-deep in a bog in a desolate section of the North York Moors; or running through the night on trails using head torches and feeling the warmth of the sun on your face as it rises at 4 a.m., don't tend to be the experiences of an average road runner.

Fell and mountain running takes place all over Britain and Ireland on steep, uneven ground where the hills are part and parcel of the experience. The Fell Runners Association categorises races by the amount of ascent and descent, from walkers' classes to the highest MM, or mountain marathon, which are multi-day events – often in bleak, wild areas – where competitors have to carry all their food and camping equipment.

> *American Terrence Stanley holds the record for the longest gap between winning the same race twice, having won the Erie Marathon in 1977 and again in 2005.*

There are many different types of running and racing experiences on offer to athletes of all abilities. Stepping outside of your comfort zone and trying a new type of running event could open a new world of adventure, travel and fun. If you don't try, you will never know what you are missing.

24-hour fell-running challenges in Britain and Ireland

The Ramsay Round, Scotland

Twenty-four summits over 56 miles (90 km), with climbs of around 28,500 ft including Britain's highest peak (Ben Nevis) and 23 Munros (which are climbs of over 3,000 ft).

The Bob Graham Round, England

Runners have to bag 42 separate Lakeland peaks on a fixed circuit over 72 miles (116 km).

The Paddy Buckley Round, Wales

A circular route over 62 miles (100 km), taking in 47 summits, and including Snowdon and the Carneddau mountain range, starting and finishing in Llanberis, where the separate Snowdon Marathon also finishes.

The Wicklow Round, Ireland

Another looped course, over 62 miles (100 km) long and with a punishing 6,000 m of climbing. The route was run by Eoin Keith on the 30 May 2009 in an astonishing 17:53:45, over 1:45 quicker than the previous record.

CHAPTER 10

THE 5s AND 10s

What distinguishes those of us at the starting line from those of us on the couch is that we learn through running to take what the days gives us, what our body will allow us, and what our will can tolerate.

JOHN BINGHAM, RUNNER AND AUTHOR

Back in the day

By the time of the XV Olympiad in 720 BC, a third foot race called the *Dolichos* was introduced to the still-limited athletic programme. Historians believe it to have been between 18-24 laps of the stadium at Olympiad, amounting to around 5,000 m. Competitors started and finished in the stadium, with the middle section run in the grounds, passing statues such as Nike near the temple of Zeus. It seems a version of Nike has been with the Olympic Games ever since. The 5,000 m predates almost every modern racing distance, with the marathon not even making the podium until 1896.

The Flying Finns

The 10,000 m first appeared in the 1912 Olympics. In this and the Games that followed, the event was dominated by a succession of runners from Finland nicknamed 'the Flying Finns', who took five golds out of a possible six, with the great Paavo Nurmi collecting two medals eight years apart. The Finns' domination extended to the 5,000 m, with Hannes Kolehmainen being the first man to double up and win both events at the same Games. Nurmi won silver in 1920 and 1928, and gold in 1924 with a new world record. Ville Ritola won silver in 1924 and gold in 1928. Lauri Lehtinen took gold in 1932 - with Lauri Virtanen taking bronze - and silver in the next Games behind Gunnar Höckert. The war interrupted their dominance and the Finns had to wait until 1972 before Lasse Virén became the second Finn and only the fourth man in history to win double 5,000 m and 10,000 m golds at the same Games. He repeated the feat in 1976 making him the only double doubler in history.

Olympic 10,000 m gold medal winners

Women

Date	Runner	Nationality	Time
1988	Olga Bondarenko	Russia	31:05.21
1992	Derartu Tulu	Ethiopia	31:06.02
1996	Fernanda Ribeiro	POR	31:01.63
2000	Derartu Tulu	Ethiopia	30:17.49
2004	Xing Huina	CHN	30:24.36
2008	Tirunesh Dibaba	Ethiopia	29:54.66
2012	Tirunesh Dibaba	Ethiopia	30: 20.75

Men

Date	Runner	Nationality	Time
1912	Hannes Kolehmainen	Finland	31:20.8
1920	Paavo Nurmi	Finland	31:45.8
1924	Ville Ritola	Finland	30:23.2
1928	Paavo Nurmi	Finland	30:18.8
1932	Janusz Kusociński	Poland	30:11.4
1936	Ilmari Salminen	Finland	30:15.4
1948	Emil Zátopek	Czechoslovakia	29:59.6
1952	Emil Zátopek	Czechoslovakia	29:17.0
1956	Vladimir Kuts	Russia	28:45.59
1960	Pyotr Bolotnikov	Russia	28:32.18
1964	Billy Mills	USA	28:24.4
1968	Naftali Temu	Kenya	29:27.40
1972	Lasse Virén	Finland	27:38.35
1976	Lasse Virén	Finland	27:40.38
1980	Miruts Yifter	Ethiopia	27:42.69
1984	Alberto Cova	Italy	27:47.54
1988	Brahim Boutayeb	Morocco	27:21.46
1992	Khalid Skah	Morocco	27:46.70
1996	Haile Gebrselassie	Ethiopia	27:07.34
2000	Haile Gebrselassie	Ethiopia	27:18.20
2004	Kenenisa Bekele	Ethiopia	27:05.10
2008	Kenenisa Bekele	Ethiopia	27:01.17
2012	Mo Farah	Great Britain	27:30.42

Double top for the match

Extraordinarily, women didn't have a 5,000 m at the Olympics until 1996, after the 3,000 m was introduced for the first time in 1984. Tirunesh Dibaba was the first woman to win both 5,000 m and 10,000 m events at the same games, which she did in 2008. She also ran a world record of 14:11.15 in a separate race in Oslo on June 8 that year, over 25 seconds quicker than Hannes back in the day. There have been seven male doublers who have won the 5,000 m and 10,000 m at the same Games including Britain's Mo Farah in London in 2012.

Doublers – men 5,000 m gold medal winners

Date	Runner	Nationality	Time
1912	Hannes Kolehmainen	Finland	14:36.6
1952	Emil Zátopek	Czechoslovakia	14:06.72
1956	Vladimir Kuts	Russia	13:39.86
1972	Lasse Virén	Finland	13:26.42
1976	Lasse Virén	Finland	13:24.76
1980	Miruts Yifter	Ethiopia	13:20.91
2008	Kenenisa Bekele	Ethiopia	12:57.82
2012	Mo Farah	Great Britain	13:41.66

Doublers – women 5,000 m gold medal winner

Date	Runner	Nationality	Time
2008	Tirunesh Dibaba	Ethiopia	15:41.40

5 and 10 ks and the rest of us

The 5,000 m and 10,000 m are primarily track-based events. For non-professionals, their first introduction to racing is likely to be at 5 k or 10 k events, on road or trails. A 5 k race equates to 3.1 miles and is far enough to provide a challenge yet not so far as to discourage, unless someone mentions that's 14 times around an average-sized rugby pitch. Events are held all over the UK every single weekend and bank holiday, even on Christmas Day before the sherry and three-week-boiled Brussels sprouts are consumed. The Trionium Knacker Cracker 10 k on 1 January is a great hangover challenger. As the organisers say: 'You'll laugh. You'll cry. You'll hurl', and all in fancy dress.

Charles Olemus of Haiti ran the slowest 10,000 m of all time at the Olympics in 1972, finishing his heat in 42:00.11, 14 minutes behind the winner. He ran the last six laps on his own and delayed the whole track and field schedule. Another Haitian, Dieudonné LaMothe, finished last in the 5,000 m at the 1976 Olympics in Montreal.

And on every weekend thou shalt race

Let your eyes look directly forward, and your gaze be straight before you. Keep straight the path of your feet, and all your ways will be sure.

PROVERBS 4:25-26

The holy book of running, *Runner's World*, advertised 557 separate 5 k races and 852 10 k races in 2013, with a peak of 97 and 157 runs respectively in May when the summer racing season begins and the traditional marathon PB-hunting season starts to draw to a close. Experienced marathoners tend to choose races in April and October, as the heat of summer even in the UK can increase long-distance race times, whilst having less effect on shorter ones.

There are many more 5 k and 10 k events in the UK than those just advertised in *Runner's World*. In recent years, the parkrun phenomenon has swept the nation and the world. The Race for Life series, Running4Women 8 k and 10 k races and the Bupa Great Women's 10 k have given women of all abilities the chance to run or walk these distances under no pressure. Organisations like the RNLI rely on the donations from runners who enter their events. Many charities actively encourage participants to dress up and have fun whilst running. It is very entertaining for runners and spectators alike to watch 300 humans wearing antlers, a red nose and reindeer T-shirts struggling through the mud in the grounds of Woburn House in the depths of winter watched by herds of deer; or 700 Santas wearing only Speedo swimming trunks and hats in freezing weather hurtling down the road in Boston, Massachusetts. It's hard to achieve a personal best wearing a snowman costume.

> *Mike McLeod shares the record for the longest winning streak, having come first 16 times in a row in the Saltwell Harriers 10 k race.*

The parkrun community

The parkrun events are free, weekly, timed, mostly Saturday-morning 5 k runs held, at the time of writing, in 177 locations around the UK, as well as venues in Australia, Denmark, Iceland, Ireland, New Zealand, Poland, South Africa and the USA. Founded by Paul Sinton-Hewitt in 2004, the first parkrun (or Bushy parkrun, named after the location of the inaugural race in Surrey) saw just 13 runners take part. The aim was not to create a series of races but rather runs where people could turn up and do whatever they wanted, with the emphasis on taking part. The brilliantly simple concept allows – as its website states – athletes of any ability to run with Olympians, veterans to show a clean pair of Achilles heels to juniors and the opportunity for non-club runners to dip their unblackened toenails into low-key fun events. To join the growing throng, a runner pre-registers, prints their own specific barcode and turns up at the event of their choice. No queues to collect numbers, pens to be herded into or warm-up routines to undertake with Mr Motivator. Afterwards, a quick flash of the barcode to one of the waiting volunteers and then it's off to the coffee shop for a well-deserved skinny cappuccino. Results appear magically on each run's webpage later in the day, with every runner's specific data updated with each new run.

It's a way of life for many, with Saturday mornings inextricably linked to the run, a chance to catch up with friends – or overtake them – and that all-important social cappuccino forgetting the pressures of life for a few brief moments. Sinton-Hewitt, who was awarded a Heroes of Running Award by *Runner's World* in 2009, couldn't have foreseen the success of his brainchild. In one run alone, in Brighton & Hove in September 2012, 499 runners took part, more than some club-organised races. By March 2013, the ever-changing weekly stats recorded that 258,042 runners in the UK alone had taken part in 15,784 events with 2,109,401 separate runs reaching 10,547,005 km, totalling 106 years, 267 days, 8 hours, 17 minutes and 57 seconds. The parkrun central database doesn't provide average race times, although it does update the fastest male, female, most first places, average runs per athlete and PBs, providing the more serious and casual runner alike with the chance to monitor their progress. To encourage runners, they have clubs for runners who reach 50, 100 and 250 parkruns, as well as a ten-race club for juniors. It is inspiring to see families taking part, eight-year-olds keeping up with their parents, parkrun tourists and 80-somethings strutting their stuff.

More pain please?

Running is like mouthwash: if you can feel the burn it's working.
BRIAN TACKETT, ATHLETE

Don't be deceived into thinking shorter distances are easy, particularly if a personal best is on the menu. Most runners will eventually experience the pain of racing in some form or other, no matter what their distance or pace. One person's energy threshold might not be reached until mile 20 of a marathon, whilst another's might be in the middle of a 5 k race. When reached, the feeling of exhaustion, legs so heavy that it's difficult to put one foot in front of the other and lungs bursting at the seams will make the finish line appear even further away than it is. Varying the race distance will affect the level and type of discomfort.

The 'gasping for breath' feeling is very specific to 5 k races. In the same way, the depletion of carbohydrates and the explosion of lactic acid in the legs at the 'wall' is inextricably linked to a marathon. Olympian Peter Maher said: 'Running is a big question mark that's there each and every day. It asks you, "Are you going to be a wimp or are you going to be strong today?".' Enlightened amateur athletes know that running isn't about beating others, it's about doing the best they can. The 'pain is temporary and glory lasts forever' saying should read 'and glory lasts until the next race', when another shiny medal can be added to the trophy cabinet that all runners secretly have at home. Any runner who has experienced the discomfort of a race and who joins the start line of another, should recite the words of runner and author Dr George Sheehan: 'I have met my hero and he is me.'

CHAPTER 11

HALF MARATHONS

*Running is the greatest metaphor for life because
you get out of it what you put into it.*

OPRAH WINFREY, US CHAT SHOW HOST

Half history

A half marathon is 21.0975 km (13.1094 miles), run primarily on roads or trails. It has taken many years for the distance to be standardised, as it did the marathon. In 1898, the Kungsbackaloppet race in Sweden was 27 km and in 1927 Stockholm was 25 km. A 15-mile race started in Waiatarua, New Zealand, in 1943. Races in Kanaguri Hai Tamana, Japan, in 1949 and Paderborner Osterlauf, Germany, in 1950 were both 20 k. The Bernie Hames race in England in 1957 was close at 21.05 k. By the 1960s, races began appearing on the circuit that were the standard distance, like Route du Vin in Luxembourg, San Blas in Puerto Rico and Caesar Rodney in the USA, followed in the 1970s by Hallwilerseelauf in Switzerland. During that decade, the USA in particular witnessed an unprecedented growth in accurately measured races.

In subsequent decades, the half marathon has grown in popularity around the world. In 2000, the GöteborgsVarvet race in Sweden had an estimated world record 79,719 finishers. By 2013, *Runner's World* advertised 293 races in the UK alone, with many more not on their list.

Some of the larger events offer facilities for wheelchair athletes to race, such as the Great North Run, which saw Canada's Josh Cassidy claim a hat-trick of victories in the 2012 event. Britain's Paralympic athletes David Weir and Shelly Woods had previously won the event four times each.

On 7 April 2013, 91-year-old Mike Fremont set a world record for his age, running the Knoxville Half Marathon in a time of 3:03:56 to add to the world record he holds for the same age group in the marathon with a time of 6:35:47 set in November 2012.

The distance is a challenge, which requires training and commitment, but not at the level of a marathon. It's not so all-consuming, is less daunting than a full marathon and post-race recovery is quicker. Whilst both distances continue to grow in participation numbers, the half marathon is out-sprinting its rival both in the UK and the USA.

The Great North Run

Former elite athlete Brendan Foster created the largest half marathon in the UK, which was run on 28 June 1981, when 12,000 runners took part in the inaugural event that was won by local man and Olympian Mike McLeod. It has grown to become one of the largest races in the world and attracts national television coverage. In 2012, 55,000 entrants were accepted out of 100,000 applicants, all seeking to run from Newcastle, across the Tyne Bridge and on to South Shields. Along the way, they were treated to a Red Arrows air display, numerous bands and the unwavering support of the crowd that lined the route. Many who run the race do so for charity or in memory of friends and family who have passed away. All are likely to remember the top-class organisation, world-class athletes, the final mile along the seafront and the camaraderie among the runners every step of the way.

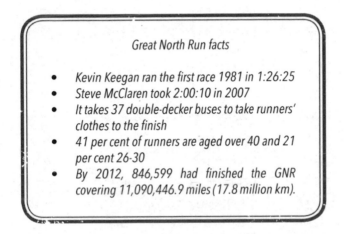

Great North Run facts

- *Kevin Keegan ran the first race 1981 in 1:26:25*
- *Steve McClaren took 2:00:10 in 2007*
- *It takes 37 double-decker buses to take runners' clothes to the finish*
- *41 per cent of runners are aged over 40 and 21 per cent 26-30*
- *By 2012, 846,599 had finished the GNR covering 11,090,446.9 miles (17.8 million km).*

Winners of the Great North Run

Men

Year	Runner	Nationality	Time
2012	Wilson Kipsang	Kenya	59:06
2011	Martin Mathathi	Kenya	58:56
2010	Haile Gebrselassie	Ethiopia	59:33
2009	Martin Lel	Kenya	59:32
2008	Tsegay Kebede	Ethiopia	59:45
2007	Martin Lel	Kenya	1:00:10
2006	Hendrick Ramaala	South Africa	1:01:03
2005	Zersenay Tadesse	Eritrea	59:05
2004	Dejene Berhanu	Ethiopia	59:37
2003	Hendrick Ramaala	South Africa	1:00:01
2002	Paul Kosgei	Kenya	59:58
2001	Paul Tergat	Kenya	1:00:30
2000	Faustin Baha	Tanzania	1:01:51
1999	John Mutai	Kenya	1:00:52
1998	Josiah Thugwane	South Africa	1:02:32
1997	Hendrick Ramaala	South Africa	1:00:25

Year	Runner	Nationality	Time
1996	Benson Masya	Kenya	1:01:43
1995	Moses Tanui	Kenya	1:00:39
1994	Benson Masya	Kenya	1:00:02
1993	Moses Tanui	Kenya	1:00:15
1992	Benson Masya	Kenya	1:00:24
1991	Benson Masya	Kenya	1: 01:28
1990	Steve Moneghetti	Australia	1:00:34
1989	El Mostafa Mechchadi	Morocco	1:02:39
1988	John Treacy	Ireland	1:01:00
1987	Robert de Castella	Australia	1:02:04
1986	Mike Musyoki	Kenya	1:00:43
1985	Steve Kenyon	Great Britain	1:02:44
1984	Oyvind Dahl	Norway	1:04:36
1983	Carlos Lopez	Portugal	1:02:46
1982	Mike McLeod	Great Britain	1:02:44
1981	Mike McLeod	Great Britain	1:03:23

Winners of the Great North Run (cont.)

Women

Year	Runner	Nationality	Time
2012	Tirunesh Dibaba	Ethiopia	1:07:35
2011	Lucy Kabuu	Kenya	1:07:06
2010	Berhane Adere	Ethiopia	1:08:49
2009	Jessica Augusto	Portugal	1:09:08
2008	Gete Wami	Ethiopia	1:08:51
2007	Kara Goucher	USA	1:06:57
2006	Berhane Adere	Ethiopia	1:10:03
2005	Derartu Tulu	Ethiopia	1:07:33
2004	Benita Johnson	Australia	1:07:55
2003	Paula Radcliffe	Great Britain	1:05:40
2002	Sonia O'Sullivan	Ireland	1:07:19
2001	Susan Chepkemei	Kenya	1:08:40
2000	Paula Radcliffe	Great Britain	1:07:07
1999	Joyce Chepchumba	Kenya	1:09:07
1998	Sonia O'Sullivan	Ireland	1:11:50
1997	Luciana Subano	Kenya	1:09:24

Year	Runner	Nationality	Time
1996	Liz McColgan	Scotland	1:10:28
1995	Liz McColgan	Scotland	1:11:42
1994	Rosanna Munerotto	Italy	1:11:29
1993	Tegla Loroupe	Kenya	1:12:55
1992	Liz McColgan	Scotland	1:08:53
1991	Ingrid Kristiansen	Norway	1:10:57
1990	Rosa Mota	Portugal	1:09:33
1989	Lisa Martin	Australia	1:10:43
1988	Grete Waitz	Norway	1:08:49
1987	Lisa Martin	Australia	1:10:00
1986	Lisa Martin	Australia	1:09:45
1985	Rosa Mota	Portugal	1:09:54
1984	Grete Waitz	Norway	1:10:27
1983	Julie Barleycorn	Great Britain	1:16:39
1982	Margaret Lockley	Great Britain	1:19:24
1981	Karen Goldhawk	Great Britain	1:17:36

On 13 January 1979, a six-way tie for first place in 1:04:46 was declared in the Governor's Cup Half Marathon.

The runner's high

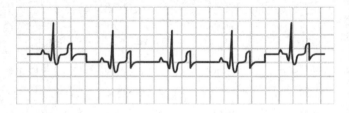

Running long and hard is an ideal antidepressant, since it's hard to run and feel sorry for yourself at the same time. Also, there are those hours of clear-headedness that follow a long run.

MONTE DAVIS, RUNNER

Running can help people with mild depression and anxiety as it provides a sense of purpose, opens new horizons and gives that magic feel-good factor. One study has reported an increase in anxiety levels in new runners, although after a month many reported a marked reduction in their perceived levels of stress. Pre-running lows are swapped for post-run highs, believed by some to be caused by the production of endorphins through exercise and by others through achieving a particular goal that had been set. Author Adharanand Finn said, 'After a run you feel at one with the world, as though some unspecified, innate need has been fulfilled.'

The average addicted mile-muncher doesn't need a medical degree to know that the runner's high is addictive, whatever the biological or physiological cause. Once achieved, a runner will want it again and again. It is an extremely exciting time in the lead up to that first race entry, with all the fears, hopes and uncertainties it brings. It's hard to be down when adrenaline is being produced at high levels.

Current world records recognised by the International Association of Athletics Federations for the half marathon are (men) Zersenay Tadese in 58:23 and (women) Mary Jepkosgei Keitany in 1:05.50.

UK road half-marathon record reductions

Men

Time	Runner	Date	Race location
1:01:03	Nick Rose	15 September 1985	Philadelphia, USA
1:01:14	Stephen Jones	11 August 1985	Birmingham, England
1:01:39	Geoffrey Smith	25 September 1983	Dayton, USA
1:02:36	Nick Rose	14 October 1979	Dayton, USA
1:02:47	Anthony Simmons	24 June 1978	Welwyn Garden City, England
1:03:40	Trevor Wright	08 April 1978	The Hague, Netherlands
1:03:53	Derek Graham	02 May 1970	Belfast, Northern Ireland

Women

Time	Runner	Date	Race location
1:06:47	Paula Radcliffe	07 October 2001	Bristol, England
1:08:42	Liz McColgan	11 October 1992	Dundee, Scotland
1:09:15	Liz McColgan	05 May 1991	Exeter, England
1:10:59	Liz McColgan	12 October 1986	Dundee, Scotland
1:12:07	Ann Ford	06 April 1986	Reading, England
1:12:31	Paula Fudge	04 April 1982	Fleet, England
1:13:07	Kathryn Binns	01 August 1981	Dartford, England

CHAPTER 12

MARATHONS

*We are different, in essence, from other men. If you
want to win something, run 100 metres. If you want
to experience something, run a marathon.*

EMIL ZÁTOPEK, OLYMPIAN

History

The standard marathon distance is 42.195 k or 26 miles and 385
yards, commonly referred to as 26.2 miles.

The race appeared for the first time in competition over 40 km
on 10 April 1896 at the Olympic Games, when 14 Greeks and four
foreigners set off to win a silver cup donated by a French philologist,
Michel Bréal. Nine finished that first race, which was won by Spyridon
Louis. Women weren't allowed to run – and would not have their own
Olympic marathon for another 88 years – although reports from the
time indicate that two women named Melpomene and Stamathis
Revithi shadowed the men all the way. Unfortunately, no official
records were kept.

Marathons haven't always been the now-standard distance and
initially tended to be around 25 miles, or 40 km. One notable exception
was the 1904 St Louis Olympic marathon, which proved to be longer

due to inaccurate course measurement. The Missouri City Marathon has, since 2000, put on a yearly accurate race without any reported hitchers claiming top spot (as Fred Lorz had in the 1904 race).

> *The Stavros Niarchos Foundation in Athens bought the cup won by Spyridon Louis for a reported $878,000 in 2012.*

The world's oldest marathon

The Olympic Committee's spectacle was quickly adopted as the event of choice by the Boston Athletic Association, as part of its aim 'to encourage all manly sports and promote physical culture'. The BAA put on its first 39 k marathon in 1897 and it has continued to this day, missing only one race in 1917, making it the oldest race on the circuit. It is many distance athletes' destination race, provided they can make the high qualifying entry standards. In order to gain entry, men aged 34 and under have to have run a previous marathon quicker than 3:05:00 and women 3:35:00, with the qualifying time increasing for runners over 80 up to 4:55:00 for men and 5:22:00 for women. The high qualification standard means that unlike New York City or London, there is less chance of being overtaken by a giant red phone box or a panda. The terrorist acts at the 2013 race shocked runners across the globe. The aftermath bore testament to the strength of the human spirit, and the compassion of runners and spectators alike.

Top ten oldest marathons

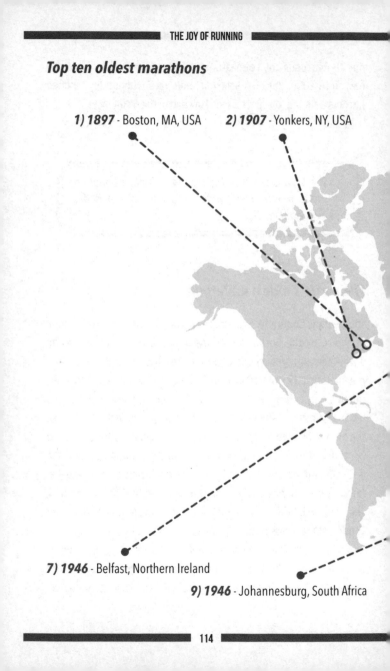

1) 1897 - Boston, MA, USA

2) 1907 - Yonkers, NY, USA

7) 1946 - Belfast, Northern Ireland

9) 1946 - Johannesburg, South Africa

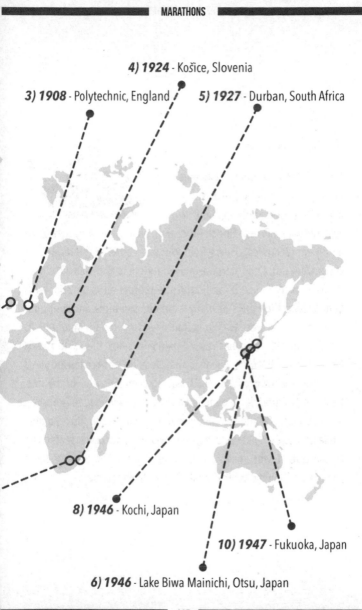

4) 1924 - Košice, Slovenia

3) 1908 - Polytechnic, England   **5) 1927** - Durban, South Africa

8) 1946 - Kochi, Japan

10) 1947 - Fukuoka, Japan

6) 1946 - Lake Biwa Mainichi, Otsu, Japan

By royal decree

The 1908 London Olympic marathon was due to finish at the new White City Stadium, built to coincide with a Franco-British exhibition, on an accurately measured 41.84 km (26 miles) course from Windsor Castle. At the request of Queen Alexandra, the start was moved further back to allow children in the nursery to see it, adding in the process an extra 388 yards and dashing the hopes of many would-be sub-three and four-hour runners in the process. The distance was eventually adopted as standard in 1921 and has caused pain ever since. The 1908 race is also famous as the great Italian runner Dorando Pietri collapsed yards from the finish when in the lead. Having been helped over the line, he was subsequently disqualified and the race awarded to American Johnny Hayes. The sense of British fair play won over in the end and, while he wasn't reinstated, Pietri was awarded a specially created cup by the Queen, who may have felt a little guilty. The extra distance conquered even the professionals. There's hope for us all.

Sunday-morning fever

Marathon running as a recreational pastime spread slowly around the globe. In Africa the Comrades Marathon started in 1921, whilst in Asia the Fukuoka began in 1947. Races sprang up, but they weren't the mass-participation events they are now. In Britain, the Polytechnic Marathon started in 1908 and has been run intermittently since. Others followed, including Ryde on the Isle of Wight in 1957 and White Peak in 1977 – which has a steep, painful downhill section around the 23-mile (37 km) mark – but races were sporadic. It wasn't until the London Marathon in 1981 that long-distance running really started to appeal to the wider British public and only then after a slightly wobbly start.

London's calling

*Every jogger can't dream of being an Olympic champion,
but he can dream of finishing a marathon.*
FRED LEBOW, NEW YORK CITY MARATHON ORGANISER

The success of the New York City Marathon inspired Chris Brasher to repeat the vision of Lebow in Britain. Brasher had been mesmerised by the New York City race and wrote about it in the *Observer* newspaper, calling it the 'greatest folk festival the world had seen'. The people of New York had taken the race to their hearts and would come out in their thousands to support the runners. Anyone who has run the race can testify to the generosity of support along the course. The wall of sound that seems to emanate particularly along 1st Avenue, where  the spectators can be ten deep, can be a highly emotional experience. It was this that Brasher sought to replicate. He wanted to raise the standard of British marathon running, give athletes of any size, speed or ability the chance to enter, unite people and create a lasting sporting event for the city.

On 29 March 1981, 7,055 runners, of whom 300 were women, started the first race and 6,255 finished in cold, wet conditions. It was a dead heat between American Dick Beardsley and Norwegian Inge Simonsen in 2:11:4, with Joyce Smith winning the women's race in a British record time of 2:29:57.

What makes London so special? Every single runner and supporter that turns out, and the atmosphere they create. Try catching a 6.30 a.m. train into the City on race day. The excitement bubbles over into animated conversations on normally silent commuter trains, many rehearsing race plans or discussing how many jelly babies to eat at mile 12 or 17.4. What to drink and when (water and sports drinks at different times), what to Vaseline (everything), what to wear (old worn-in gear), how fast to run the first 3 miles (planned and practiced race pace), how many loo stops (shouldn't need them if hydrated properly), pre-race rituals (four visits to the portables) and more are all minutely dissected.

Guinness World Record marathon times achieved at London in 2012 include David 'Dracula' Stone with 2:42:17, the fastest marathon runner dressed as a fictional character; and George and Charley Phillips the fastest marathon runners on stilts with 6:50:02.

Slower, ordinary, determined people run in a race with the world's best. They wear Elvis costumes, aim for PBs or just try to finish, or not be outpaced by a hotdog with legs and have feet too painful to walk on for days. Yet every single finisher will share a sense of achievement and pride. They will enjoy the fun, the feeling of being part of one huge running family and the satisfaction that all those months of training have paid off, whatever their finishing time. It feels as though the crowds are cheering every step of the way and, for the most part, they are.

When Olympian Sohn Kee-Chung said, 'The body can do so much. Then the heart and spirit must take over', he might have been describing his 1936 Olympic win, but that applies equally to every marathoner who has ever stood on a start line. Finding the spirit and will to continue when everything hurts (including the bits not Vaselined properly) is an admirable quality. 'You have to forget your last marathon before you try another. Your mind can't know what's coming', said Frank Shorter. Even the pros hurt and that's what makes the marathon such a personal achievement.

Weird science

Good nutrition is essential for athletic performance and energy is gold. Carbohydrates are the body's most accessible energy source, which is stored as glycogen. Humans can hold enough for around 90–120 minutes of intense exercise, mostly in the muscles and liver. Once gone, the body turns to its fat reserves, which are much less efficient at converting to energy, and hey presto, your legs feel like tree trunks and race pace is very hard to maintain.

When this happens, it's said that you have hit the fabled 'wall'. The rate of reduction of stored levels can be slowed through use of carbohydrate-based gels or sports bars during races and increased levels of fitness. In ultras, particularly of the Long Distance Walkers Association kind, gels and the like are swapped for sandwiches, sausage rolls and cakes. Runners convert glycogen to energy aerobically and anaerobically. The distance specialists train for the former, with LSD (long slow distances) designed to push up their lactate-producing threshold and build aerobic endurance, whilst sprinters like Usain Bolt train for short-term explosive power. If Bolt tried running a marathon without changing his training, the chances are he would fall apart and hit the 'wall' like an untrained amateur.

Africa – the marathon continent

As at the time of writing, the 47 quickest legal men's marathons have been run by either a Kenyan or Ethiopian. Out of the top 345 times, only 67 go to runners from other countries. The only British runner in the list is Steve Jones, who ran a PB at the Chicago Marathon in 1985. Kenyan or Ethiopian women hold 150 of the top 348 slots, although only appear three times in the top ten. British women fair much better than their male counterparts, with Paula Radcliffe holding the top three fastest times ever and a total of nine runs in the list, with Mara Yamauchi and Véronique Marot appearing once each.

Grand Slam – the 'Six Nations'
current fastest marathon times

France
2:06:36 - Benoît Zwierzchiewski - 6 Apr 2003 - Paris

Wales
2:07:13 - Steve Jones - 20 Oct 1985 - Chicago

Italy
2:07:22 – Stefano Baldini - 23 Apr 2006 - London

England
2:08:33 - Charles Spedding - 21 Apr 1985 - London

Scotland
2:09:16 - Allister Hutton - 21 Apr 1985 - London

Ireland
2:11:23 - John Treacy - 12 Feb 1990 - Tokyo

Big business

Marathon running on a global scale is now a huge, lucrative business. With the ease of access to many of the world's races, the number of participants and finishers continues to rise. In 2011, the New York City Marathon had 46,795 finishers and London had 36,672. In 2010, Chicago had 36,159, whilst Berlin had 35,786 in 2008 and Tokyo 33,328 in 2011. It's difficult to pinpoint why only 23 finished the Crawley Marathon in 2010, where competitors had to run 105 times around a 400 m running track.

Marathon running hasn't become easier. The distance throws up the same challenges as it has since 1908. Average race times, save in a few categories, are declining due to the availability and accessibility of races leading to record entries and finishers.

Perhaps some have adapted Henry V's speech to provide extra motivation to enter:

> *And gentlemen in England now a-bed*
> *Shall think themselves accursed they were not here,*
> *And hold their manhoods cheap whiles any speaks*
> *That ran with us upon London Marathon day.*

MAD, BAD AND DANGEROUS RACES

Some of the world's greatest feats were accomplished by people not smart enough to know they were impossible.

DOUG LARSON, AUTHOR

6633 Extreme Winter Ultra Marathon

This six-day 350-mile (563 k) race starts at Eagle Plains, Yukon, Canada, on the Dempster Highway, before entering into the Arctic Circle after 23 miles (37 k) at the latitude of 66 degrees and 33 minutes, through the Northwest Territories to Inuvik, with a final 120 miles (193 k) along the ice road to Tuktoyaktuk on the shores of the Arctic Ocean. It claims to be the 'toughest, coldest and windiest extreme ultra marathon on the planet', with some justification. Runners are self-sufficient and have to pull sleds with all their gear. Checkpoints only offer water and shelter. Given some are 70 miles (113 k) apart, it's unlikely Domino's will deliver if someone forgets their tin opener. In 2013, only four out of 20 entrants finished in perishing temperatures that can reach -44°C. The bite-sized fun run version at 120 miles (193 k) had five finishers out of six entrants. All had to battle against frostbite and hypothermia, dodge aircraft landing on the highway and try not to get lost in the frozen wastelands.

Trail of Tears 5 k

What's different about this 5 k trail race near to Route 66 and Tulsa, Oklahoma, is the fact that runners wear shoes, socks and nothing else other than a bit of strategically placed Vaseline. Getting back to nature and 'social nude recreation' is the aim of the race. It is one in a series organised by the American Association for Nude Recreation, which includes the Sahnoan Bare Buns Run 5 k, Skinnydipper Sun Run 5 k, Road Kill Run and Bare As You Dare. Racers are ironically presented with race T-shirts and medals, although where they hang them is always a difficult question to ask.

Comrades Marathon

This 56-mile (90 k) road race between Pietermaritzburg and Durban in the KwaZulu-Natal province, South Africa, is the oldest ultra race in the world, the first one having  taken place on 24 May 1921. The direction of the race is alternated each year between the two cities, creating 'up and down' years, due to the changes in elevation. It attracts thousands of runners and supporters every year, with 19,545 entering in 2012.

It is a cruel race. Competitors have to run the course in under 12 hours to be allowed to finish, and receive an official time and medal. One second outside the limit and it's gone for another year. It's televised live in South Africa and the last-placed person is celebrated as much as the winner.

The Jungle Marathon

Set in the Amazon rainforests, this 254 k (157 mile) race is the direct opposite of the  6633. Temperatures climb as high as 43°C, with 90 per cent humidity and some of the creepiest crawlies on the planet. In 2012, 63 runners from 15 different nations battled snakes and avoided jaguars, whilst enduring very steep, muddy climbs and dense jungle trying to find easily missable trails. They crossed swamps and tried not to be eaten by piranhas, all whilst carrying a week's worth of supplies. There are also 42 k (26 miles) and 122 k (75 miles) options. Not one for the barefoot running brigade.

The Antarctic Ice Marathon (half and full)

Set inside the wilderness of the Antarctic, both races require competitors to face average wind-chill temperatures of -20°C, constant light, and powerful katabatic winds that can reach 300 km (186 miles) per hour. It's too cold even for the penguins, whose march stopped many miles back. Even

getting to the start is an adventure dependent on the weather, as the place is officially the coldest on the planet (the lowest temperature ever recorded was -89°C at the Russian Vostok research station).

Ultra-Trail du Mont-Blanc

Arguably the greatest of all mountain races, the UTMB takes place in the stunning Mont Blanc Massif over a 168 km (105 mile) course with 9,600 m of ascent. It runs through France, Switzerland and Germany, has a maximum number of 2,300 competitors and a cut-off time of 46

hours. There is so much climbing that even mountain goats think twice about following the competitors. It's hard to even enter, as competitors require seven qualification points that can only be amassed by entering other designated trail ultra-distance runs. The organisers do allow these to be accumulated over two years, but even then, entry to the race isn't guaranteed due to the popularity of the event.

> *Between 2008 and 2011, Kílian Jornet Burgada won the race three times and holds the current course record of 20:36:43; the one year he didn't win, the race was cancelled.*

Runners carry a designated kit list. Oxygen bottles aren't compulsory despite having to climb the Grand Col Ferret, which at 2,537 m is the race's highest peak. Any race where the winner comes in 24 hours ahead of the last-placed competitor is going to be a toughie. If you train for months on end and think you are fit enough for this bad boy, train a few months more and you still won't be.

The Beer Mile

More of a subculture than a race, the concept of the Beer Mile is simple. Run four fast laps of a track and drink four pints of beer. The challenge grew in university campuses in America, although a brief search of YouTube confirms British students have adopted the challenge with some gusto. As it's not recognised by the IAAF or any athletic governing body, the unofficial rules are not set in tablets of stone. In general they are as follows:

Each runner must drink a can of beer before the start of each lap

Beer must be consumed within a 10 m transition area at the race start/finish

Standard cans not less than 355 ml or 12 oz are used and must be opened in the transition area

Vomiting during the challenge incurs an extra lap penalty.

In the same vein, the Shamrock 5 k Beer Run in Indianapolis, Indiana, tempts runners with a beer every kilometre and medals that double as bottle openers. Given the 10 a.m. start, an afternoon nap is often required after the run.

The Self-Transcendence 3,100 Mile Race

*There is only one perfect road, and that road is
ahead of you, always ahead of you.*
SRI CHINMOY, INDIAN SPIRITUAL TEACHER

This is the world's longest footrace. The event takes place in Queens,
New York, every year over 52 days between June and August. Runners
average 60 miles every single day, looping a city block measuring
0.883 km (0.5488 miles) a staggering 5,649 times. Great for the
spectators, although tedious for the runners, the record is currently
held by German Madhupran Wolfgang Schwerk, who in 2006
reached 3,100 miles in 41 days 8:16:54.

Created by Chinmoy in 1997 – who upped the distance from the previous year's 2,700 miles as clearly that wasn't far enough – his philosophy is: 'The expression of self transcendence – going beyond personal limits and reaching new levels of inner and outer perfection. Whether it be in the athletic world or any endeavor, for someone to transcend his previous achievements is inner progress and an expression of a new determination, which can only bring us closer to our destined goal – real satisfaction.'

Competitors run the risk of disqualification if they run under 50 miles a day, with a mandatory six-hour curfew imposed by race officials – who probably want to sleep.

Marathon des Sables

Another multi-day event that calls itself the 'toughest footrace on earth', the Marathon des Sables is a very difficult six-day race in the Sahara Desert in Morocco. Created in 1986 by Patrick Bauer, runner's sweat evaporates before they feel it due to the stifling heat, with temperatures reaching over 38°C. It is broken down into six stages of differing lengths:

- Stage 1 – 29 km (18 miles)
- Stage 2 – 35.5 km (22 miles)
- Stage 3 – 40 km (24 miles)
- Stage 4 – 82.2 km (51 miles)
- Stage 5 – 42.2 km (26 miles)
- Stage 6 – 21.1 km (13 miles)

The athletes have to carry their own kit, be self-sufficient and have a minimum of 14,000 calories worth of food. In reality, they will need much more than that. Even the mandatory kit list is a sign of just how dangerous this race can be. Runners have to take at least the following:

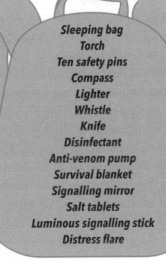

Sleeping bag
Torch
Ten safety pins
Compass
Lighter
Whistle
Knife
Disinfectant
Anti-venom pump
Survival blanket
Signalling mirror
Salt tablets
Luminous signalling stick
Distress flare

As Morocco is home to 12 different species of snake, ten scorpions and a number of spiders, the survival kit really could mean the difference between life and death. Add in heat, blisters covering what seems to be the entire foot, poor food, total exhaustion, sand that rips open any chafing injury and disorientation and this really is one the world's hardest footraces.

In 1994, Italian police officer and former reserve in the Italian Olympic marathon team of 1984, Mauro Prosperi got lost and ended up wandering the desert. He was found nine days later over 100 miles off course, having lost 30 lb in body weight. Naturally, having come close to death in the race, he subsequently returned to run it seven more times. Sadly, the race claimed the lives of two other runners in the years that followed Prosperi's close call, including an apparently fit Bernard Julé who died of a heart attack in 2007 following the long stage in which he came 45th out of 750 competitors.

The Olympic rower James Cracknell achieved 12th place in the 2010 race, giving him the highest finish yet for a Brit. Ozzy Osborne's son Jack foolishly attempted to run the race on little training, for his television show *Adrenaline Junkie*. Predictably, he dropped out some way before the end. Rock on, Jack.

CHAPTER 14

ULTRAS

People can't understand why a man runs. They don't see any sport in it. Argue it lacks the sight and thrill of body contact. Yet, the conflict is there, more raw and challenging than any man versus man competition. For in running it is man against himself, the cruellest of opponents. The other runners are not the real enemies. His adversary lies within him, in his ability, with brain and heart to master himself and his emotions.

GLENN CUNNINGHAM, US OLYMPIAN

History

An ultra marathon is in essence any distance beyond a standard marathon. Common race distances run are 100 miles (160 k) and 62 miles (100 k) events. Historic ultras were often multi-day indoor track events, popular in Britain and America in the 1870s, run between a Monday and Saturday. Races were commonly known as 'wobbles' and competitors 'pedestrians'. An event of this type is described in Peter Lovesey's book *Wobble to Death*. The six-day races and ultra running in general eventually lost the public's interest and for a number of years events were scaled down.

> In 1882, Charles Rowell ran 300 miles on an indoor track in 58:17:06 – a time that has never been beaten.

By the 1920s, interest in the ultra was again rising. In South Africa, the first Comrades Marathon took place in 1920 and the Transcontinental Footrace took place in 1928 in the United States. For many years, ultra running was not undertaken by the masses. Judging by the number of ultra events that now take place in the UK, it seems that this extreme end of the sport has never been more popular.

Why?

To many runners, a marathon is quite rightly seen as their Ben Nevis, an enormous and yet achievable endeavour. For some non-professional, recreational athletes the distance is just not far enough. Once traversed a number of times, the excitement of a marathon can wane and the endorphins crave bigger challenges. The only way for some to rediscover the buzz is to do something they think they might just be able to do but are not sure – just as they felt when they entered their first marathon. Few runners forget the electrifying mix of nerves, excitement, anticipation and the sense of possibility felt on that first starting line. To recapture that can lead to ever-longer races being entered, as one distance after another is achieved.

The mind of an ultra runner is moulded by what they have achieved in the past. Very few runners step straight into monster mile-munching without having earned their stripes by conquering the marathon first. Once that particular beast has been vanquished, thoughts turn to the next mountain to climb – and the days when 26.2 miles seemed a long way fade into the subconscious, as ever-increasing distance runs take over.

At the 26.2 mile point of an ultra, as runners pass the standard marathon distance, they might be wise to consider the words of Winston Churchill: 'This is not the end. It is not even the beginning of the end. But it is, perhaps, the end of the beginning.' The relevance of those stirring words is dependent on the length of the ultra, as distances vary with every race. A runner covering a smaller ultra, such as the 34-mile (54 k) Greensands Ridge event held in Bedfordshire each June, will see the marathon distance as the penultimate focus point of the whole run. An ultrateer running the Montane Lakeland 100-mile (161 k) race, held each July in the Lake District, dare not contemplate it as even the end of the beginning. For very long races, the mind needs to be focused on achievable short-term goals and not the glory of the final sprint finish, 74 miles (119 km) away. Your grey matter cells must be trained to think, and believe, that even running past the marathon point is nothing special. Sixty per cent of an ultra is in the training; 30 per cent in the mind. The rest is left to avoiding rabbit holes, wrong turns and trying to digest all manner of nutritionally bereft foodstuffs to keep you going.

The world's longest-running ultra marathons

Race	Distance	Location	Year started
Comrades	89 km (56 miles)	Durban, South Africa1	921
Pieter Korkie	50 km (31 miles)	Germiston, South Africa	1948
London to Brighton	88 km (55 miles)	Brighton, England	1951
Saint Etienne–Lyon	70 km (43 miles)	Lyon, France	1952
Bieler Lauftage	100km (62 miles)	Biel, Switzerland	1959

Just a short 26.2 miles today?

A marathon for the really long ultra boys and girls will turn into a Saturday-morning training run. Anyone fit and determined enough to take on any ultra has to learn to lose focus on the immediate miles ahead. They have to treat the distance with both respect and disdain in equal measure. The running icon Walt Stack said: 'Start slowly and taper off', although he should have also added 'walk the hills'. There is no hiding place in an ultra, no helpful course marshal to push you along when you fade. If you haven't put the miles in and trained properly, you will be found out. Respect the race with proper, focused training in the months leading up to it. Having put the miles in the bank, stick your chest out and tell it that 30, 40 or even 70 miles isn't far and you are going to beat it. If an ultra runner believes that 30 miles is a long way, they are in the wrong arm of the sport. If they see the last 30 miles as the homeward leg, next year they will be queuing up qualifying points for the Ultra-Trail du Mont-Blanc.

Exceptions to the rule

There are runners who defy rules and expectations. They might not be famous or known beyond their club, yet their achievements deserve to be heard. Rebecca Fleckney is one such runner who, prior to her club's inaugural 84-mile non-stop John Bunyan trail run, had never run more than a marathon. The event was designed to allow club members to run any distance they wanted between 1 and 84 miles. She set out with the intention of making maybe 40 miles and ended up covering the lot in a very creditable 24:21:19. How did she do it? By focusing on the next checkpoint and not thinking about how far to go. When she arrived at mile 40, she decided to go to the next checkpoint and then the next until she was so close, no one would let her stop even if she wanted to. She hadn't trained her body for the rigours of that distance but she was able to control her mind.

Where does it end?

> *It hurts up to a point and then it doesn't get any worse.*
> ANN TRASON, US ULTRA RUNNER

There will come a point, even on the Herculean ultrateer's radar, where the distances become daunting. In one recent 104-mile (167 k) event, the author casually asked a fellow runner how they were finding it. 'Taking it easy,' came the reply, as 'I have a 200 miler in four weeks and this is a training run for that.' There is always someone dafter than you out there. Always.

STATS

The oldest road races in the world

According to the Association of Road Racing Statisticians (ARRS), the following is a list of the ten oldest recorded footraces in the world:

Race name	Distance	Location	Year commenced
Palio del Drappo Verde	10 km	Verona, Italy	1208
Red Hose Race	3 km	Carnwath, Scotland	1509
Kanto Road Race	10 miles	Narita, Japan	Not known
Christmas Day Handicap Challenge	5 miles	Rotherham, England	1888
Clonliffe Harriers Road Race	2 miles	Dublin, Ireland	1891
Delaware YMCA Turkey Trot	8 km	Buffalo, USA	1896
Boston Marathon	26.2 miles	Boston, USA	1897 – 2012
Bechovice-Praha	10 km	Prague, Czechoslovakia	1897
Kungsbackaloppet Half Marathon	13.1 miles	Gothenburg, Sweden	1898 – 2012
Prague-Brandýs nad Labem	15 km	Brandýs nad Labem, Czechoslovakia	1893

Progression of 5,000 m world record

Men

Time	Runner	Nationality	Race location	Date
12:37.35	Kenensia Bekele	Ethiopia	Hengelo, Netherlands	31 May 2004
12:39.36	Haile Gebrselassie	Ethiopia	Helsinki, Finland	13 June 1998
12:39.74	Daniel Komen	Ethiopia	Brussels, Belgium	22 August 1997
12:40.18	Kenensia Bekele	Ethiopia	Paris Saint-Denis, France	1 July 2005
12:41.86	Haile Gebrselassie	Ethiopia	Zurich, Switzerland	13 August 1997

Women

Time	Runner	Nationality	Race location	Date
14:11.15	Tirunesh Dibaba	Ethiopia	Oslo, Norway	6 June 2008
14:12.88	Meseret Defar	Ethiopia	Stockholm, Sweden	22 July 2008
14:16.63	Meseret Defar	Ethiopia	Oslo, Norway	15 June 2007
14:20.87	Vivian Jepkemoi Cheruiyot	Kenya	Stockholm, Sweden	29 July 2011
14:22.51	Vivian Jepkemoi Cheruiyot	Kenya	Oslo, Norway	15 June 2007

Progression of 10,000 m world record

Men

Time	Runner	Nationality	Race location	Date
26:17.53	Kenensia Bekele	Ethiopia	Brussels, Belgium	26 August 2005
26:20.31	Kenensia Bekele	Ethiopia	Ostrava, Czech Republic	8 June 2004
26:22.75	Haile Gebrselassie	Ethiopia	Hengelo, Netherlands	1 June 1998
26:25.97	Kenensia Bekele	Ethiopia	Eugene, USA	8 June 2008
26:27.85	Paul Tergat	Kenya	Brussels, Belgium	22 August 1997

Women

Time	Runner	Nationality	Race location	Date
29:31.78	Junxia Wang	China	Beijing, China	8 September 1993
29:53.80	Meselech Melkamu	Ethiopia	Utrecht, Netherlands	14 June 2009
29:54.66	Tirunesh Dibaba	Ethiopia	Beijing, China	15 August 2008
29:56.34	Elvan Abeylegesse	Turkey	Beijing, China	15 August 2008
29:59.20	Meseret Defar	Ethiopia	Birmingham, England	11 July 2009

Progression of half-marathon world record

Men

Time	Runner	Nationality	Race location	Date
58:22	Zersenay Tadese	Eritrea	Lisbon, Portugal	21 March 2010
58:30	Zersenay Tadese	Eritrea	Lisbon, Portugal	20 March 2011
58:33	Samuel Wanjiru	Kenya	The Hague, Netherlands	17 March 2007
58:46	Mathew Kisorio	Kenya	Philadelphia,USA	18 September 2011
58:47	Atsedu Tsegay	Ethiopia	Prague, Czech Republic	31 March 2012

Women

Time	Runner	Nationality	Race location	Date
1:05:50	Mary Keitany	Kenya	Ras Al Khaimah, United Arab Emirates	18 February 2011
1:06:09	Lucy Kabu	Kenya	Ras Al Khaimah, United Arab Emirates	15 February 2013
1:06:11	Priscah Jeptoo	Kenya	Ras Al Khaimah, United Arab Emirates	15 February 2013
1:06:25	Lornah Kiplagat	Netherlands	Udine, Italy	14 October 2007
1:06:27	Rita Sitienei	Kenya	Ras Al Khaimah, United Arab Emirates	15 February 2013

Progression of marathon world record

Men

Time	Runner	Nationality	Race location	Date
2:03:38	Patrick Musyoki	Kenya	Berlin, Germany	25 September 2011
2:03:42	Wilson Kiprotich	Kenya	Frankfurt, Germany	30 October 2011
2:03:59	Haile Gebrselassie	Ethiopia	Berlin, Germany	28 September 2008
2:04:15	Geoffrey Kiprono Mutai	Kenya	Berlin, Germany	30 September 2012
2:04:16	Dennis Kimeto	Kenya	Berlin, Germany	30 September 2012

Women

Time	Runner	Nationality	Race location	Date
2:15:25	Paula Radcliffe	Britain	London,England	13 April 2003
2:17:18	Paula Radcliffe	Britain	Chicago, USA	13 October 2002
2:17:42	Paula Radcliffe	Britain	London, England	17 April 2005
2:18:20	Liliya Shobukhova	Russia	Chicago, USA	9 October 2011
2:18:37	Mary Keitany	Kenya	London, England	22 April 2012

World junior marathon records per age year

Age	Time	Name	Nationality	Date	Race location
5yrs 358dys	5:25:09	Bucky Cox	USA	4 Jul 1978	Junction City, OR, USA
6yrs 341dys	4:07:27	Bucky Cox	USA	17 Jun 1979	Toledo, OH, USA
7yrs 195dys	4:04:08	Wesley Paul	USA	6 Sep 1976	Columbia, MO, USA
9yrs 325dys	2:56:57	Wesley Paul	USA	16 Dec 1978	Huntsville, AL, USA
10yrs 211dys	3:02:23	Daven Chun	USA	15 Dec 1974	Honolulu, HI USA
11yrs 323dys	2:47:17	Wesley Paul	USA	13 Dec 1980	Huntsville, AL, USA
12yrs 364dys	2:46:42	Wesley Paul	USA	24 Jan 1982	Houston, TX, USA
13yrs 146dys	2:43:02	Tom Ansberry	USA	15 Jan 1977	San Diego, CA, USA
14yrs 233dys	2:42:30	Chang-Son Kim	North Korea	30 Nov 1966	Pnom Penh, Cambodia
15yrs 225dys	2:29:11	Mitch Kingery	USA	13 Feb 1972	Burlingame, CA, USA
16yrs 359dys	2:15:07	Zhu-hong Li	China	15 Oct 2000	Beijing, China
17yrs 357dys	2:10:46	Zhu-hong Li	China	14 Oct 2001	Beijing, China

Progression of 100 km world record

Men

Time	Runner	Nationality	Race location	Date
6:13:33	Takahiro Sunada	Japan	Tokoro, Japan	21 June 1998
6:16:41	Jean-Paul Praet	Belgium	Winschoten, Netherlands	12 September 1992
6:17:17	Takahiro Sunada	Japan	Belvès, France	30 April 2000
6:18:09	Valmir Nunes	Brazil	Winschoten, Netherlands	16 September 1995
6:18:24	Mario Ardemagni	Italy	Winschoten, Netherlands	11 September 2004

Women

Time	Runner	Nationality	Race location	Date
6:33:11	Tomoe Abe	Japan	Yubetsu, Japan	25 June 2000
7:00:27	Norimi Sakurai	Japan	Winschoten, Netherlands	08 September 2007
7:00:48	Ann Trason	USA	Winschoten, Netherlands	16 September 1995
7:09:44	Ann Trason	USA	Amiens, France	25 September 1993
7:10:32	Tatyana Zhyrkova	Russia	Winschoten, Netherlands	11 September 2004

Largest number of marathon finishers

Finishers	Marathon	Date
46,795	New York City	6 November 2011
44,829	New York City	7 November 2010
43,633	New York City	1 November 2009
38,557	New York City	4 November 2007
37,936	New York City	5 November 2006

Largest number of finishers in a race for all years it has run

Finishers	Marathon
923,228	New York City
815,953	London
605,764	Berlin
582,648	Honolulu
555,459	Paris

CONCLUSION

There has never been a better time to be an athlete than right now. Poor old Pheidippides didn't have the advantages of today's runners and he paid the penalty. We have at our fingertips easily accessible nutritional advice, training plans and support from a multitude of social-media websites. Advances in specialist clothing, training shoes for every terrain, satellite-navigation watches, hydration packs and pocket-sized gadgets that carry 10,000 songs all make a runner's life a lot easier. All we have to do is head out the door and find a route, race or challenge. There are different running events in Britain, and abroad, every single weekend of the year. We can take part in events involving thousands of people, head for the trails and revel in splendid isolation or join a team of friends as they wade through mudbaths trying not to be electrocuted. Or we can just leave the gadgets behind and simply run; whenever or wherever we want. That's the real Joy of Running.

KEEP

ON

RUNNING

THE HIGHS
& LOWS OF A
MARATHON ADDICT

Phil Hewitt

Keep on Running
The Highs and Lows of a Marathon Addict

Phil Hewitt

ISBN: 978 1 84953 236 5   Paperback   £8.99

Marathons make you miserable, but they also give you the most unlikely and the most indescribable pleasures. It's a world that I love – a world unlocked when you dress up in lycra, put plasters on your nipples and run 26.2 miles in the company of upwards of 30,000 complete strangers.

Phil Hewitt, who has completed over 20 marathons in conditions ranging from blistering heat to snow and ice, in locations from Berlin to New York, sets a cracking pace in this light-hearted account of his adventures on the road. This story of an ordinary guy's addiction to running marathons looks at the highs and lows, the motivation that keeps you going when your body is crying out to stop, and tries to answer the ultimate question, 'Why do you do it?'

'This is a wonderful and frank view of a first-time-marathoner-turned-running-addict. Phil shares the pitfalls and emotions that running a marathon for the first time evoke and how running can grab you and draw you back for more'

LIZ YELLING, Double Olympian and Commonwealth bronze medallist

'An intriguing insight into one man's marathon journey… an inspiring read for any marathoner or wannabe marathoner'

ANDI JONES, International long-distance runner

'Phil Hewitt's well written account of his marathon-running addiction (he's up to 25) takes us from his home town of Chichester to the concrete canyons of New York. … This is the story of a man in love with his sport. … For those of us fitting running in between job, family and everything else life has to throw at us, this is definitely a book you will make a connection with'

MEN'S RUNNING Magazine, November 2012

THE JOY OF CYCLING

RAY HAMILTON

THE JOY OF CYCLING

Ray Hamilton

ISBN: 978 1 84953 457 4   Hardback   £9.99

Be at one with the universe. If you can't do that, at least be at one with your bike.

LENNARD ZINN

This pocket-sized miscellany, packed with fascinating facts, handy hints and captivating stories and quotes from the world of cycling, is perfect for anyone who knows the incomparable joy of bikes.